A Passion For
SPECIALTY
PAPER

More Than 50 Clever Techniques for Scrapbooking

Brandi Ginn and Pam Klassen

MEMORY
MAKERS
BOOKS

Denver, Colorado

AUTHORS AND ARTISTS Brandi Ginn and Pam Klassen
MANAGING EDITOR MaryJo Regier
EDITOR Emily Curry Hitchingham
ART DIRECTOR Nick Nyffeler
GRAPHIC DESIGNERS Jordan Kinney, Robin Rozum
ART ACQUISITIONS EDITOR Janetta Abucejo Wieneke
CRAFT EDITOR Jodi Amidei
PHOTOGRAPHER Ken Trujillo
CONTRIBUTING PHOTOGRAPHERS Lizzy Creazzo, Jennifer Reeves
EDITORIAL SUPPORT Karen Cain, Amy Glander, Dena Twinem

Memory Makers® A Passion for Specialty Paper

Published by Memory Makers Books, an imprint of F+W Publications, Inc.
12365 Huron Street, Suite 500, Denver, CO 80234
Phone (800) 254-9124
First edition. Printed in the United States.
10 09 08 07 06 5 4 3 2 1

Library of Congress Cataloging-in-Publication Data

Klassen, Pam.
    A passion for specialty paper: more than 50 clever techniques for scrapbooking / by Pam Klassen & Brandi Ginn.
        p. cm.
    ISBN 1-892127-61-X
        1. Photograph albums. 2. Photographs--Conservation and restoration. 3. Scrapbooks. 4. Paper work. I. Ginn, Brandi. II. Title.

TR465.K543 2005
745.593--dc22

2005054017

Distributed to trade and art markets by
F+W Publications, Inc.
4700 East Galbraith Road, Cincinnati, OH 45236
Phone (800) 289-0963
ISBN 1-892127-61-x

Distributed in Canada by Fraser Direct
100 Armstrong Avenue
Georgetown, ON, Canada L7G 5S4
Tel: (905) 877-4411

Distributed in the U.K. and Europe by David & Charles
Brunel House, Newton Abbot, Devon, TQ12 4PU, England
Tel: (+44) 1626 323200, Fax: (+44) 1626 323319
E-mail: mail@davidandcharles.co.uk

Distributed in Australia by Capricorn Link
P.O. Box 704, S. Windsor NSW, 2756 Australia
Tel: (02) 4577-3555

Memory Makers Books is the home of *Memory Makers*, the scrapbook magazine dedicated to educating and inspiring scrapbookers.
To subscribe, or for more information, call (800) 366-6465. Visit us on the Internet at www.memorymakersmagazine.com.

First and foremost, this book is dedicated to our families who once again lived through piles of laundry, pork-and-bean dinners and sinks full of dishes—all on our behalf for our love of scrapbooking. We sincerely love and thank you.

We would also like to recognize the countless designers in this industry who motivate us to be better artists each day. We are inspired by your ingenuity every time we create.

To all the readers who are challenged by using specialty papers: We hope that you will be inspired by the ideas in this book to unlock the potential of your own creativity.

table of contents

4
LEATHER PAPERS
36–43

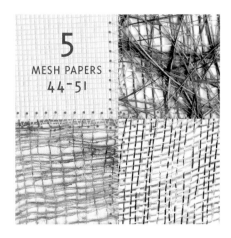

5
MESH PAPERS
44–51

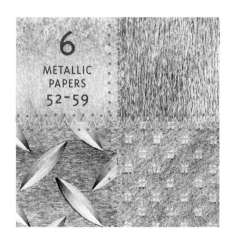

6
METALLIC PAPERS
52–59

7
NATURAL PAPERS
60–67

8
TEXTURED PAPERS
68–75

9
TRANSPARENT PAPERS
76–83

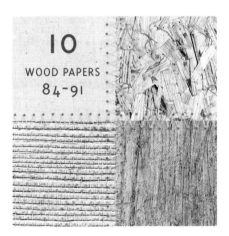

10
WOOD PAPERS
84–91

Introduction

In creating this book, we were thrilled at the opportunity to immerse ourselves in the world of specialty papers in order to learn how to effectively incorporate them into scrapbook design. It was a process even for experienced artists like us, but after months of challenging our creativity, we discovered unique looks that can be achieved with the use of these beautiful papers. Through our exploration, we learned that each type of specialty paper possesses its own distinct qualities with colors, textures and patterns that can create highly individual designs. As we handled each paper, we wondered about its origin and creation. In all, we discovered much about the art of paper making—an ages-old process rich in history.

Paper is the most widely used material for writing and drawing around the world. Ancient Egyptians, Greeks and Romans first used the material papyrus, from which paper derives its name. Early techniques such as "tapa" involved spreading cooked pulp across a screen frame that was then allowed to dry in the sun. Once dry, the sheet would then be pulled off the screen for use.

The birth of modern paper as we know it began in 105 A.D. at the hands of Ts'ai Lun, a Chinese court official who invented paper making from textile waste using rags. Paper-making techniques were introduced in 610 A.D. to Japan and Korea, at which point the process of working with pulp yielded characteristics of what we now refer to as mulberry paper. Over the next several hundred years, paper-making techniques evolved and divided. Some industry craftsman were known as "smoothers" while others were known as "stampers." Each sect refused to recognize the other as full-fledged paper makers. With the development of factory-made papers in the 17th century, the production of handcrafted papers was reduced. The 19th and 20th centuries ushered in the biggest increase in paper making, with production times growing from 5 meters per minute in 1820 to over 500 meters per minute in 1930.

With today's renewed interest in artistic communication through crafts and scrapbooking, there has been a revival of beautiful paper designs and artistic handmade papers—as well as the introduction of archival quality materials. As each paper is unique, experimentation will be invaluable before beginning projects in this book. We've taken some of the guesswork out for you so that wasting materials with such experiments won't be necessary. Each chapter features step-by-step instructions for intermediate to advanced techniques, creative ideas for attaching the papers, as well as ways to create the look of each specialty paper featured using supplies you may already have on hand.

We'll show you how to transform specialty papers into amazing projects utilizing such popular techniques as paper tearing, layering, stitching, folding, pleating and much more. Join us in exploring the endless possibilities in the world of specialty papers.

Be passionate...

Brandi
Pam

Brandi Ginn and Pam Klassen
Authors and artists

Illustrated Tips and Techniques

The techniques shown here are designed to help you achieve the best possible results when creating works of art with specialty papers. Ideally, your work space should be clean and uncluttered—but creative chaos works too! Cover your surface with a self-healing cutting mat and work with clean, sharp tools.

1

Crease and burnish papers with a bone folder to easily achieve a clean, folded line.

2

Cut fabric using a rotary cutter, self-healing mat and a ruler to produce edges without fraying. Free-form curves can be cut without a ruler.

3

Various looks and textures can be achieved when working with fuzzy papers. The natural nap of the paper is smooth and lighter in color. If the paper is pulled against the nap, a rough, darker texture is revealed.

4

Pre-poke holes into leather paper with an awl and hammer for easier stitching.

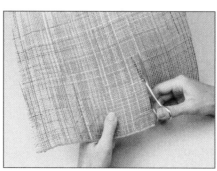

5

Easily produce a straight cut in mesh paper by following the lines of the weave.

6

Run sheets of metal through a hand-held crimper to create great texture.

7

Use a water brush to draw a straight line in natural paper to aid in gently pulling the loose fibers apart. Once dry, the raw edges maintain the integral look of the paper.

8

Vellum paper can be torn both against the grain and with the grain. Tearing against the grain creates a bumpy, uneven edge, while tearing with the grain produces a straight edge.

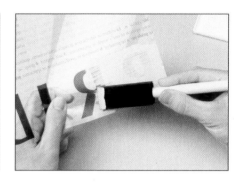

9

Paint on the back of printed transparencies to provide contrast to the text and allow it to be more visible on the page.

10

The distinctive nature of wood paper will absorb liquid to create an unusual texture. Walnut ink provides a great contrasting color.

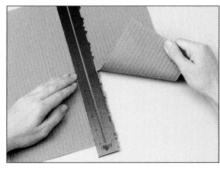

11

Tear paper along a deckle-edge ruler. The result is an evenly torn edge that follows a straight line.

12

Add a blanket stitch to fabric paper to finish the raw edge. The stitch provides a soft contrasting design to the paper.

Tools

When working with specialty papers, there are a few must-have tools to make your creations easier to design—many of which may already be part of your scrapbook stash. Additional products and advanced tools may be needed to complete specific projects. Pictured below are those items most regularly used.

TIP

To preserve your creations permanently, always choose archival-quality products to fill your scrapbooks. Select albums and paper products that are acid- and lignin-free, and adhesives and colorants that are photo-safe. If questionable paper products will be included in your scrapbook, coat with a spray-on acid neutralizer.

BASIC TOOLS:

Self-healing cutting mat

Rotary cutter

Paintbrushes

Spray adhesive

Double-sided tape

Acid-free spray

Brayer

Tape runner

Craft knife and replacement blades

Hammer

Eyelet setter

Adhesive dots

Scissors

Un-Du adhesive remover

Scoring tool—bone folder/burnisher

Liquid glue

Rulers—metal/clear/grid

ADDITIONAL TOOLS:

Awl

Baby wipes

Circle cutters

Crimper

Deckle ruler

Embossing stylus

Hole punch

Iron

Needle and thread

Palette knife

Punches

Sandpaper

Sea sponges

Sewing machine

Templates

Paper trimmer

Needle-nose pliers

Organization and Storage

The storage and organization of specialty papers requires some thoughtful planning. All papers are best stored in a cool, dry place with an ideal temperature of no more than 75 degrees. Make sure to keep the papers out of direct sunlight and high humidity to avoid any fading or warping. Protect your investment by handling your papers with care. Be mindful of exposed edges that could become bent or torn, and be sure your hands are clean and dry before handling.

Papers squeezed tightly within a storage environment are a disaster waiting to happen. For example, embossed or cobblestone papers should be loosely stored to avoid crushing the pattern or texture. Thick mesh or riveted papers have the potential of damaging neighboring papers with which they are stored by leaving indentations. Storage for delicate mesh papers works best when each sheet is separated by a paper liner or cardstock, allowing for easy removal. Softer papers such as fabric, handmade, mulberry and wood papers with less rigidity should be stored with supports. The surface of high gloss and metallic papers can potentially become scratched, so these papers should be kept separate from coarse textured papers. Vellum papers are particularly sensitive to heat and moisture. Exposure to either will cause the paper to warp.

First and foremost, find what works best for you! The goal is to not waste time looking for papers that should be readily available for creating masterful works of art. Below are some ideas to get you started.

A few companies supply a wide range of specialty papers, so sorting by manufacturer can allow you to easily find coordinating papers. This vertical paper storage system by Cropper Hopper reinforces papers that would otherwise droop or bend. Four smaller paper pouches fit within a large holder, providing ample support for papers. Coarse mesh papers are strong enough to stand on their own within this system. Separating your collection of specialty papers by colors gives you the option to mix diverse patterns and textures.

An inexpensive skirt/pant hanger is a great way to visibly display papers. It allows you to see several sheets at a time and can serve double-duty as wall décor hanging from hooks. Be mindful of papers that may become damaged by the clamp—try covering clamps with felt to protect the papers from indentations.

Some of the most beautiful papers available come in oversized sheets that prove a bit more challenging to store. Hanging papers over dowel rods with eye hooks screwed into each end and hung from chains is a safe and easy solution. The wooden rod should either be painted or covered with fabric to eliminate any transfer of lignin from the rods to the papers.

PAPERS

BATIK
JAPANESE CHIYOGAMI
PRINTED
MARBLED

Although decorative art papers made their debut hundreds of years ago, the beauty of these ages-old designs can still inspire modern scrapbooking. The silky elegance of a shimmery Japanese print, the beautiful individuality of a batik design, the hand-painted quality of print block papers and the one-of-a-kind beauty of marbled papers—each can inspire countless unique creations.

These light- to medium-weight papers can be cut with any kind of scissors, craft knife or rotary cutter and also tear easily to produce soft edges. Although beautiful, not all art papers are considered archival and should not directly touch photos or memorabilia without the use of a de-acidification spray. Specific adhesives may be needed in order to maintain the integrity of the paper. Tape runners may pull off a layer of paper. Adhesive dots or double-sided tape work particularly well. The porous nature of these papers provides an ideal surface for paint and ink, but beware of busy patterns, as they may not be ideal for accommodating stamped or embossed images. Art papers are durable enough to machine- and hand-stitch and are beautiful when used for folding and layering. Journaling can easily be added by hand or with the use of a computer.

You may feel that art papers are too beautiful to use in your scrapbooks, but with a little experimentation and the ideas in this chapter to inspire you, you will learn ways to pleat, stitch, tear and layer exquisite art papers in your pages.

THE SWEET FRUITS OF SUMMER

Pam Klassen

Photos: Ryan Watamura, Reedley, California

SUPPLIES: Fruit, feather papers (Papers by Catherine);
brown, pink Japanese Washi papers (PaperGami); Marble Turquoise/
Apricot/Raspberry paper (Graphic Products Corp.); dusk emboss/apple
green paper (Ex-Imp Global); rub-on letters (Me & My Big Ideas); metal
embellishment (Artchix Studio); adhesive (Therm O Web); ribbon

Stitch art papers

Use a variety of art papers and machine-stitch a geometric pattern across the top to create a unified mix of patterns. Cut a variety of squares and rectangles from art papers. Adhere to background page. Draw a random geometric pattern across the top of papers and machine-stitch through all thicknesses. Mat photos and adhere to background. Print title and journaling and add rub-on letters to title blocks. Silhouette cut feathers and adhere to page. Use paint to color metal embellishment. Add ribbons and adhere to page.

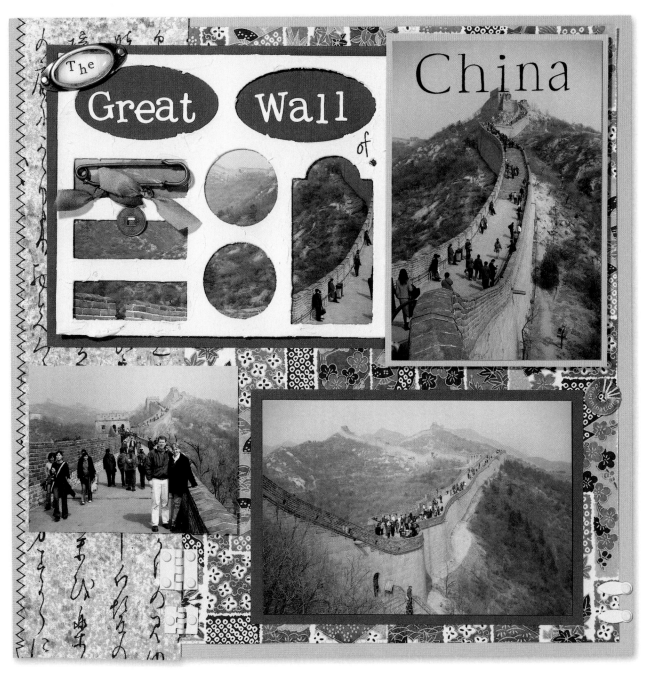

THE GREAT WALL OF CHINA
Brandi Ginn
Photos: Pete Spransy, Salt Lake City, Utah

SUPPLIES: Japanese Washi paper (PaperGami); textured
cardstock (Bazzill); embellishment frame (Chatterbox); label
holder, letter stickers, rub-on letters, hinges, photo turns,
washer, acrylic paint (Making Memories); safety pin, Chinese
coin (Jewelry Shoppe); letter stickers (Doodlebug Design);
adhesive (Therm O Web); silk ribbon

Creative attachments for art papers

Here stitching, hinges and photo turns provide subtle but artistic touches for attaching art papers to the
page background. Place two Japanese Washi papers on the background and machine stitch a zigzag
pattern along one side. Attach hinges at the paper seams and place photo turns at the bottom right.
For a fun twist on photo framing, spread modeling paste over a repurposed product packaging element, allow to dry and add color with acrylic paint to create texture found in the featured photos. Layer
finished frame over a matted photo and embellish with safety pin and metal label holder. Create the title
using letter stickers, a concho and rub-on letters.

BUTTERFLY PAVILION

Brandi Ginn

SUPPLIES: Thai Batik butterfly paper (Graphic Products Corp.); textured cardstock (Bazzill); chipboard letters, tag, date stamp, rub-on letters (Making Memories); letter stamps (Hero Arts); frame, photo corner (Heidi Swapp); acrylic ribbon charm (Junkitz); adhesive dots (Therm O Web); ribbon

Decoupage with batik paper

Create a soft design using specialty paper that thematically enhances your photos. Tear batik paper and machine-stitch to pink cardstock. Group photos together on one side and accent with oversized photo corners. Frame a portion of one photo with an acrylic frame embellished with ribbon and rub-on letters. Paint the negative portion of chipboard letters with acrylic paint and decoupage batik paper on the positive letter elements. Use letter stamps and ribbon to further embellish the chipboard letters. Thread ribbon through an acrylic charm and adhere to the bottom of the page. Add journaling with a black pen.

N

Brandi Ginn

SUPPLIES: Japanese Washi papers (PaperGami); frame (Pottery Barn Kids); metal letters, acrylic paint, flower (Making Memories); silver jump ring, heart stamp (Heidi Swapp); pink jump ring (Junkitz); ribbon (American Crafts, May Arts); SuperTape adhesive (Therm O Web)

Create monogram letters

Artfully placed photos carry the eye to layered monograms that create an eclectic design within a shadow box frame. Alternate black-and-white and color photos along top and left side of a shadow box frame. Print the mirror image of various-sized letters on the back of an assortment of papers. Paint the negative image of a chipboard letter with pink paint, line with patterned paper and accent with ribbon. Hang a painted letter charm from jump rings tied to a chipboard letter. Paint metal accents with white and pink paints and adhere to the background.

TIP

Asian papers are very fragile and delicate. When printing on the back of the papers, use temporary adhesive to affix the paper on printer paper before printing. It's helpful to change the color of the text to gray so the ink doesn't show through the paper.

SWEETPEA
Pam Klassen

SUPPLIES: Charisma/hot pink floral paper (Ex-Imp Global); textured cardstock (Bazzill); vellum (Autumn Leaves); stamp (Uptown Design Company); adirondack alcohol paint (Ranger) rub-on letter (My Mind's Eye); stickers (K & Company); gem (Mrs. Grossman's); charm (Paper Para-chute); adhesive (Therm O Web); spray adhesive (Krylon); ribbon

Create your own faux batik paper

Create the look of batik paper using stamps, bleach, wax and paints. Follow instructions on page 17 to create the look of batik paper. Tear strips from the edges of pink floral paper. Ink the torn edges and adhere to the corners of the background page. Cut a vellum frame and adhere to the page with spray adhesive. Cut cardstock squares and add rub-on letter, flower, letter stickers, ribbon and charm. Mount photo and adhere to page. Hand journal around the edge of vellum frame.

How to create the look of batik paper

1
Dip stamp in bleach, allowing excess bleach to drip off. Stamp paper. Allow paper to dry completely. Bleach will continue to work as long as it is wet.

2
Use a white candle to draw wax over random areas of the stamped image. Waxed areas will resist the water-based paint.

3
Paint over the entire page. Allow to dry.

WALL ART

Pam Klassen
Photos: Ryan Watamura, Reedley, California

SUPPLIES: Indian Sewn papers/chain links olive, Thai screen printed Unryu/Climbing Vines green paper, Japanese Ogura Pink Taffeta lace paper (Graphic Products Corp.); Japanese Washi papers (PaperGami); apple green/sparkle, jade green/autumn leaves paper (Ex-Imp Global); photo canvas (Paper Palette); double-sided adhesive (Therm O Web); wooden frames

Create wall art

Cover wooden frames with art paper and printed photo canvas to create an artistic wall collage. Build wooden frames with ¾" boards. Miter corners. Construct the following sizes: three 9 x 6½", two 4½ x 6½", one 6 x 6½" and one 3 x 6½". Use double-sided tape on the back of the frames. Stretch papers over the frames and adhere. Cut strips of accent papers to stretch across some of the frames. Print photos on sticky-back canvas and adhere to frames.

LOVE

Brandi Ginn

SUPPLIES: Cocoa Waffle textured cardstock (Creative Imaginations); Double Espresso Cobblestone paper (FiberMark); Japanese Washi paper (PaperGami); chipboard letters, clear flowers, pink tape, jump rings, foam stamp (Heidi Swapp); ribbon (American Crafts); file label (Avery); acrylic paint (Making Memories); charm (Blue Moon Beads); SuperTape adhesive (Therm O Web)

Combine papers

Cover dimensional letters with various papers for a multitextured, multipatterned title—and for a refreshing punch of pattern and color. Trace the reverse image of each letter on several papers and cut out with a craft knife. Adhere the paper to the letters with decoupage glue and smooth flat with a brayer. Embellish letters with ribbon. Stamp a decorative accent with paint in the upper right corner of the page. Cut frame from chipboard and cover with cobblestone paper. Accent with ribbon, charm and file label.

We took advantage of our time in China while we were traveling for business. We hired a guide and went to the Forbidden City and the Great Wall. Both outside and inside the Forbidden City were enormous bronze statues. There were architecturally interesting buildings adjacent to a temple we visited in the city of Nan Chang. Whenever we travel I like to get pictures of things that are unique to that place. I wish I knew more about the things in these photos, but we were simply tourists taking pictures of interesting things we wanted to remember and show our children when we got home.
January 2005

JOURNEY TO CHINA
Brandi Ginn
Photos: Pete Spransy, Salt Lake City, Utah

SUPPLIES: Japanese Washi paper (PaperGami); textured cardstock (Bazzill); acrylic paint, rub-on word (Making Memories); black pen (EK Success); fixative spray (Krylon); Zots, SuperTape adhesive (Therm O Web); chipboard; silk ribbon; chalk pencils

Pleat art paper

Here pleated Japanese Washi papers enhance the design and architecture found within the photos. Cut and paint strips of chipboard and place at the top of each page. See steps below and adhere pleated paper elements to each side of layout. Place a small strip of adhesive along one side of the pleated paper and adhere silk ribbon. Mat photos on cardstock and place throughout the design. Create a portion of the title with rub-on words. Hand-draw the remainder, color with chalk pencils and spray with fixative.

Create pleats in the paper by folding at various intervals. Perfect pleats are not the goal here; have fun and create an individual look.

Cut strips of cardstock and adhere them between each paper pleat.

Use a small amount of tape on the back of the pleats to secure them in place while stitching. Use a machine to create a zigzag stitch to permanently secure the pleats.

fabric

PAPERS

CANVAS
MOIRÉ
BURLAP
SUEDE
EMBROIDERY

Every day, we experience the ability of fabric to evoke distinct feelings. The silky smooth texture of moiré instills a sense of romance, while the rough feel of canvas connotes a more casual, earthy feel. Striped patterns can create a masculine look, soft florals conjure a feminine feel and the homespun look of embroidered paper makes us feel like they were specially hand-stitched just for us. It is no wonder fabrics have made their way onto the scrapbook page for the charm and nostalgia they represent.

When it comes to cutting fabric, use sharp scissors designed for fabric or a rotary cutter and a grid mat. Pinking shears can create a beautiful edge, but keep in mind that decorative scissors intended for paper are not sharp enough for cutting fabric. Craft knives and circle cutters do not work well for cutting fabrics. Tearing and fraying, however, will produce unique edges. Many of today's fabrics designed for scrapbooking have a stabilizer on the back. This gives the fabric a stiff surface that enables clean cuts without fraying. For fusing pieces of fabric together, an iron-on adhesive works more favorably than a tape runner or adhesive tabs. Stitching with a sewing machine or by hand will hold pieces together as well as embellish the surface of the page. A strong double-sided adhesive is a fine alternative to machine stitching, as some adhesive-backed fabrics may leave residue on the needle. Fabric is very porous and will absorb and spread moisture. Acrylic paints work well for painting and stamping in addition to inks and heat embossing. The stabilizer permits the fabric to easily pass through a printer and maintain a fold. Fabrics without stabilizers are lighter and can be gathered, folded, pleated, frayed and easily hand-stitched. If needed, these fabrics can also be stiffened with an iron-on interfacing.

Experiment with the many patterns and textures of fabric papers, and use the ideas in this chapter to achieve striking looks using painting, quilting, stitching and pleating techniques.

LANDON
Brandi Ginn

SUPPLIES: Mimosa canvas paper (FiberMark); vertical stripe red fabric paper (K & Company); Antelope SuedePaper (Wintech); textured cardstock (Bazzill); letter stamps (Hero Arts, Ma Vinci's Reliquary); script stamps (Hero Arts); die-cut letter (Foofala); chipboard letter, photo corner (Heidi Swapp); stamping ink (Tsukineko); brad (Making Memories); SuperTape adhesive (Therm O Web)

Use fabric to create a patterned background

Blocks and strips of striped fabric paper carry the eye throughout this page and contribute a masculine touch to the background. Stitch yellow canvas paper to brown cardstock using a sewing machine. Press stamped image into suede paper with an iron (see page 43 for instructions); adhere to canvas paper. Soak the negative image of a chipboard letter in walnut ink and distress the edges with sandpaper. Complete the title using letter stamps and a die-cut letter. Layer the chipboard on fabric and secure with strong adhesive. Stamp words on strips of cardstock with brown ink. Place photos over fabric elements and accent with a photo corner.

TIP
Soaking the chipboard in walnut ink will cause it to warp. To aid with the drying process, sandwich the letter in paper towels with a heavy book on top and leave overnight.

SMILE 4 ME
Pam Klassen
Photos: Elizabeth Friesen,
Reedley, California

SUPPLIES: Tribeca Red, Nzorfolk Rose Sunshine fabric paper (K & Company); yellow fabric paper (from Summer Swatchz collection) (Junkitz); stickers (Mrs. Grossman's); "4" sticker (Creative Imaginations); stamps (Making Memories, River City Rubber Works, Stampendous!); stamping ink (AMACO); staples (Making Memories); brads (ScrapArts); adhesive dots (Therm O Web); ribbon; button; thread

Creative attachments for fabric papers

A soft floral design is showcased in this page featuring fabrics creatively attached using a variety of techniques. Machine-stitch yellow fabric and cut flower elements to the red background with straight and zigzag stitches. Embellish the page with stickers and attach floral cutouts and painted eyelet letter with a pin. Tie ribbons through holes on the side of one photo. Cut fabric blocks for the title and use paint to stamp the letters. Sew a buttonhole at the top of one block and attach with a button sewn to the page. Use staples and brads to attach the additional blocks. Stamp name on yellow background with ink.

LOVE
Art and Photos: Kortney
Langley, Reedley, California

SUPPLIES: Vertical Stripe Red, Norfolk Rose
Sunshine, Damask Pink, Buttercup Shimmer
fabric papers (K & Company); Mimosa canvas paper (FiberMark); pink fabric swatch
(from Girl Swatchz collection), buttons, letter tiles (Junkitz); fibers, ribbons (EK Success); hearts (Making Memories); stamps
(Hero Arts, Stampendous!); double-sided
adhesive (Therm O Web); lace

Cover a frame with fabric

This romantic page features a floral
fabric-covered frame, stamped
images and a lace-edged tag.
Cover chipboard frame with fabric,
adhering on the back. Tie ribbon
around one side and create mat by
layering pink fabric behind frame.
Add printed names to ribbon and attach with eyelet. Stamp hearts along
fabric strip and adhere to page with
button. Create tag by laying lace over
black paper and topping with layers
of fringed yellow and inked pink
fabrics. Embellish with fibers, ribbons and hearts. Staple tag and ink-
treated definition text to background
page. Tie ribbon to the tops of acrylic
letters and frame. Adhere to page
with double-sided adhesive.

FRAMED BIRTH ANNOUNCEMENT
Pam Klassen
Photos: Angela Siemens,
Rosenort, Manitoba, Canada

SUPPLIES: Striped fabric paper (from Summer
Swatchz collection), buttons (Junkitz); Yellow
Burlap Stickyback fabric (Paper Palette); But-
tercup Shimmer fabric paper (K & Company);
Denimtex fabric paper (Wintech); sticker
(Provo Craft); embossing powder (Tsukineko);
adhesive (Therm O Web); ribbon; rickrack;
embroidery floss

Embroidery stitch burlap

Use machine-stitching and embroidery
to create a burlap birth announcement
keepsake. Machine-stitch background
fabrics together using a zigzag stitch,
stitching ends of ribbon into the seams.
Cut openings in yellow burlap for the
photo and buttons. Layer photo opening
with two fabric mats and machine-stitch
through all thicknesses. Sew rickrack to
the outside edge of burlap. Embroider
baby's name, date and weight at the bottom of the burlap. Attach photo behind
opening. Change the color of fabric
buttons with ink, allow to dry and tie
ribbons through centers. Attach double-
sided sticker to the background page
and cover with embossing powder; shake
off excess and heat with embossing gun.
Cut foam board to fit behind burlap piece
and adhere to the center of page, leaving
button holes recessed.

Filled with awe and wonder silly Jack says "Wow" to everything he sees.

SILLY JACK
Brandi Ginn
Photos: Kara Elmore Photography,
Kaysville, Utah

SUPPLIES: Canvas paper (Office Max); textured cardstocks, chipboard shape (Bazzill); chipboard frame, foam stamp, metal clip (Heidi Swapp); adhesive (Therm O Web)

Create your own embroidered paper

Here a custom embroidered background and a canvas-printed photo make for a fashionable fabric-inspired design. Cut diamonds from cardstock and adhere to the background. Paint the edges of cardstock with acrylic paint and create diamond pattern with paint and a foam stamp. Sand the edges of a chipboard frame and embellish with ribbon and a metal clip. Print one photo on canvas paper and layer with the frame. Cut letters from cardstock to create the title. See steps to create embroidered border.

How to create the look of embroidered paper

1
Cut diamond shapes and place along one side of the cardstock background.

2
Measure from each diamond tip to tip to find the center point. Using a pencil, mark the halfway point on each side of the diamond. Draw a 3" diagonal line, making sure that the center of the diamond is the center of your line (at 1.5"). Draw a second diagonal line to finish the "X". Place craft foam beneath the cardstock. Using a sewing ruler, pierce the paper at every other hole. Erase pencil lines.

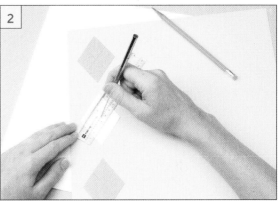

3
Sew a chain stitch along each line.

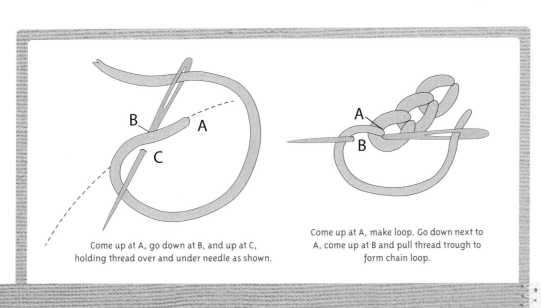

Come up at A, go down at B, and up at C, holding thread over and under needle as shown.

Come up at A, make loop. Go down next to A, come up at B and pull thread trough to form chain loop.

HOME SWEET HOME

Brandi Ginn

SUPPLIES: Woodland Crimson Toile fabric paper (K & Company); burlap paper (Creative Imaginations); transfer paper (Avery); ribbon (Making Memories); buttons

Create a fabric transfer pillow

Create a decorative accent pillow using fabric papers to brighten the décor of any room. Print the title on fabric transfer paper and follow the manufacturer instructions for transferring the words to the burlap paper. Stitch the burlap to toile paper with a contrasting color of thread. Embellish the front of the pillow with ribbon and sew buttons at each intersecting point. Cut a second piece of toile paper and machine-stitch to the back side of the pillow. Leave a small opening to insert stuffing; stitch to close.

A MOTHER'S WISH

Pam Klassen
Photos: Elizabeth Friesen,
Reedley, California

SUPPLIES: Pink floral (from Mom Swatchz) fabric paper (Junkitz); Bella, Norfolk Rose Sunshine fabric papers (K & Company); Tribal pink Thai Screenprinted Unryu paper, Cardinal red Japanese Ogura lace, Sunflower yellow Japanese Ogura lace, red/orange lace (Graphic Products Corp.); halo emboss/hot pink paper, autumn/lt. yellow (leaves) paper, adorn/red paper, Italian leather/hot pink paper (Ex-Imp Global); Coral SuedePaper (Wintech); pink floral Japanese Washi paper (PaperGami); Festive Red Maruyama paper (Magenta); Sunrise Swizzle yellow mesh, Hybiscus Pink wicker mesh (Magic Scraps); Tastefully Tattered Fabric Strips and Fabric Ties (MaisyMo Designs); ribbon, fabric words (Artchix Studio); adhesive dots (Therm O Web)

Combine papers

Brightly colored quilted blocks create the perfect backdrop for energy-filled black-and-white photos. Cut a variety of 4" squares and adhere to page. Cut strips from various papers to adhere along seams. Attach photos with glue dots. Tape and hand-stitch fabric words to background. Add self-adhesive fabric ties and word elements to pictures. Print journaling on self-adhesive transparency and adhere to top photo on page.

The ruins at the
St. Boniface Basilica

Lindsay & David's
Wedding

The
Wedding
dance

WEDDING DANCE

Pam Klassen

Photos: Angela Siemens, Rosenort,
Manitoba, Canada

SUPPLIES: Victorian Pink, Buttercup Shimmer fabric papers (K & Company);
Coral SuedePaper (Wintech); Cardinal Red Japanese Ogura lace (Graphic
Products Corp.); contour/rose embroidered paper (Ex-Imp Global); ribbon (EK
Success); beads (Halcraft); template (Crafters Workshop); stamps (Stampen-
dous!); stamping ink (AMACO); acrylic paint (Delta), leaves (Artchix Studio);
glue (Beacon Adhesives); double-sided adhesive (Therm O Web)

Embroider fabric with ribbon

Wind a ribbon throughout a fabric-adorned spread to create a romantic
design addition for wedding photos. Follow directions in steps below for
adding ribbon heart accent to both pages. Glue beads at random along
ribbon. Print text on embroidered paper and fold center edge. Place
strips of suede paper and mulberry lace between seam and attach to
pink fabric with double-sided adhesive. Mat photos on fabric, adding
mulberry lace behind two. Use a template to paint large letter on page.
Stamp remainder of title with ink. Add fabric leaf accent.

Using a pencil, trace heart pattern on fabric
background as a guide for ribbon. Cut out
center of heart.

Layer mulberry lace over suede fabric and
adhere beneath heart opening.

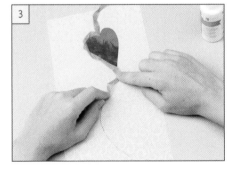

Glue ribbon to fabric, twisting to fit guide line.
Add a second ribbon at the top of the heart,
tying ends together at the bottom of the heart.
Leave one end loose and continue to glue
remaining ribbon to the bottom of page.

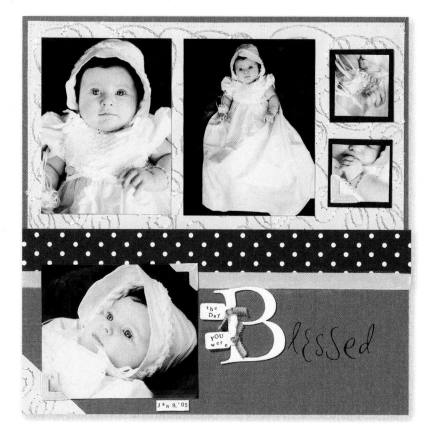

THE DAY YOU WERE BLESSED

Brandi Ginn

SUPPLIES: Contour/rose embroidered paper (Ex-Imp Global); Black Mink Caress paper (FiberMark); patterned paper (Chatterbox); tape, photo corners, chipboard letter (Heidi Swapp); file label (Avery); tags, letter stickers, rub-ons letters (Making Memories); adhesive (Therm O Web)

Use embroidered paper as a background

Here delicate embroidered papers add a feminine charm and echo the pattern found in little Natalie's dress. Stitch embroidered paper to cardstock with a sewing machine. Layer the bottom edge with patterned paper and pink tape. Crop smaller photos and mount on black paper. Accent photos with distressed photo corners and file label. Wrap a strip of embroidered paper around bottom corner of background page and secure on back. Paint a chipboard letter white and embellish with ribbon and tags. Use rub-on letters to create the remainder of the title.

NATALIE'S ROOM

Brandi Ginn

SUPPLIES: Champagne Empress Moiré paper (Wintech); pink fabric (from Girl Swatchz collection) paper (Junkitz); patterned paper (Chatterbox); chipboard letter (Heidi Swapp); paper flowers, brads, pebble letters, acrylic paint (Making Memories); SuperTape adhesive (Therm O Web)

Convert a frame with canvas paper

Create a door hanger accent by combining various papers and embellishments with a repurposed frame. Cover canvas frame with moiré paper and pink fabric. Conceal seam with patterned paper, securing on the back. Paint a chipboard letter with green paint. Print the remaining letters on canvas paper and cut with a craft knife. Place pebble letters on pink fabric. Secure paper flowers with brads and cover the outside edge with ribbon.

i WILL LoVE YOU 4Ever

little Ava,
Your my baby doll that i get
to dress up! Some day you'll
be big and want to do things on
your own For now your my little Ava.

I WILL LOVE YOU FOREVER
Brandi Ginn
Photos: Robert Woods Photography,
Layton, Utah

SUPPLIES: Norfolk Rose Sunshine fabric paper (K & Company); Vanilla Hemp fabric paper (Creative Imaginations); patterned paper, acrylic paint (Making Memories); cardstock, chipboard shapes (Bazzill); tissue paper flowers, rub-on letters, circle chipboard, photo corners (Heidi Swapp); letter stamps (Hero Arts); stamping ink (Tsukineko); embroidery floss (DMC)

Layer fabric papers

Layered textured fabrics accented with bold stitches create a nostalgic sense of feminine flair. Hand-stitch hemp paper to cardstock and layer with fabric paper. Adhere photos with a strong adhesive and accent with tissue paper flowers and photo corners. Paint chipboard shapes with yellow paint and allow to dry. Apply rub-on letters to painted chipboard and stagger to create title. Write journaling on ledger paper and attach with safety pins.

glossy & fuzzy

PAPERS

SPARKLE
MIRRORED
HOLOGRAPHIC
GLITTER

Imagine the beauty of a glitzy night out re-created on your scrapbook page. From the reflective surface of mirrored paper and the sparkle of glitter paper to the plush textures of soft fuzzy paper—any layout will benefit from the texture and dimension these papers create.

Sharp scissors will cut through the various weights and textures of these papers, but a craft knife, circle cutter and decorative scissors may only cut the gloss and sparkle papers. Tearing the papers can result in interesting edges, but some tears may need to be started with a small cut. These papers are acid-free and are therefore safe for use in your scrapbooks. Gloss and sparkle papers have an iridescent finish that makes their surfaces nonporous. Consequently, they do not easily accept ink, paints or adhesives and require stamping with solvent-based ink and computer printing that uses heat to apply the ink. While the texture of fuzzy paper is not recommended for computer printing, it can be painted. Adhesive dots or double-sided adhesives are recommended when attaching these papers. Fuzzy papers work well for hand- or machine-stitching and can easily be folded. Gloss and glitter can be attached by machine-stitching, but are hard to hand-stitch and do not fold well. Handwritten journaling will not take to these papers unless you use pens designed for slick surfaces.

Gloss, sparkle and fuzzy papers lend themselves to a variety of themes. Try using fuzzy paper for nature, sports, animal or outdoor themes. Use glitzy papers for weddings, awards and celebrations. Let's explore more fun uses in this chapter through piecing paper, photo blocks, layering and creating your own gloss, sparkle and fuzzy papers.

CLASSIC STARS
Pam Klassen
Photos: Amber Denzel, Greeley, Colorado

SUPPLIES: Funky Silver Plaid holographic paper (Grafix); Mirror Red Wyndstone paper (Graphic Products Corp.); Starlight Blue Gala mesh (Magic Scraps); orange gloss (photo paper); negative filmstrip frames (Creative Imaginations); stickers (Mrs. Grossman's, Pebbles); glitter (Magic Scraps, Sulyn); brads (K & Company); silver leafing pen (Krylon); double-sided adhesive (Therm O Web); star template

Mix glittery papers

Create a star-studded page to enhance black-and-white photos using a mix of glamorous papers. Cut three stars from orange gloss paper and back openings with silver holographic paper. Cut photos to fit transparent filmstrip frames and add words printed on transparencies. Cover star with double-sided adhesive and add glitter. Repeat for "S" and adhere to star. Create background with red gloss paper layered with glitter mesh paper, attaching with brads painted with silver leafing pen. Add sticker letters to filmstrip and filmstrip frames.

MISS J
Brandi Ginn

SUPPLIES: Jaal/red glitter paper (Ex-Imp Global); textured cardstock (Bazzill); tissue paper flower, clear flower, clear letter, heart stamp (Heidi Swapp); letter stamps, patterned stamp, ink (Hero Arts); tiles (Junkitz); rhinestones (JewelCraft); ribbon (May Arts); black pen (EK Success); Zots adhesive (Therm O Web); chalk pencils; binder clips

Creative attachments for glitter papers

Creative page additions enhance this cheery design as well as help to secure the glittery papers to the page background. Cut large circles from glitter paper and place on the background page. Layer objects around the perimeter of the circles to further secure the paper. Clamp binder clips to one side of the paper and embellish with ribbon. Stamp words with letter stamps using shadow ink and black ink. Stamp a heart with paint and place ribbon across the bottom. Create the title by hand by following the line of the circle.

NO Launch

What a disappointment! I set my alarm for 5:00am and laid in bed seriously debating whether or not I *really* wanted to get up and go see the hot air balloons take off for the Erie fair. We had gone the night before for their "Light the Night Sky" event and only a few balloons attempted to lift off but ultimately couldn't.

I finally decided it would be worth the photo op. I had been told that the balloons would be in the air by 6:30. So to be sure I got a good seat I wanted to be there before 6:00. I show up and I am literally the FIRST person on the golf course (with the exception of those who pitched tents on one of the fairways.)

Come to find out they weren't supposed to take off until after 7:00. So I waited, and waited, I watched the sun rise and waited....the wind wouldn't die down enough for the balloons to take off! I was so bummed...and extremely tired.
May 14, 2005

NO LAUNCH
Brandi Ginn

SUPPLIES: Funky Orange Sparkle, Funky Cherry Red, and Funky Green Bubbles glitter papers, transparency (Grafix); textured cardstock, chipboard shape (Bazzill); acrylic paint (Making Memories); letter stamps (Hero Arts); stamping ink (Clearsnap)

Paper piece glitter paper

This design is given a sense of flight with glitter papers that have been combined to create a hot air balloon accent. Print a clip art image on the back of various glitter papers and cut out each section. Piece them together on yellow cardstock to create balloon. Adhere photos to the page and layer one photo with strips of glitter paper attached with brads. Paint the edges of the cardstock with red paint. Paint and stamp on a chipboard shape to create part of the title. Use computer software to print the remainder of the title on a transparency and adhere to page.

DECORATIVE BOXES
Brandi Ginn
Photos: Staci Langford, Erie, Colorado

SUPPLIES: Funky Cherry Red, Funky Orange Sparkle, Funky Green Bubbles, and Funky Silver Sequins glitter papers, Funky Silver Plaid holographic paper (Grafix); paper box (Hobby Lobby); canvas paper (Office Max); textured cardstock (Bazzill); diamond stamp (Heidi Swapp); acrylic paint (Making Memories); elastic

Decorate papier-mâché boxes

Here glitter papers transformed a block of photos into visually interesting desktop art pieces. Adhere glitter paper to each side of a purchased paper box. Print photos on canvas paper, mat on black cardstock and adhere to each side of box. Poke a hole in one corner of the box, insert black elastic and tie a knot on one end. Wrap the elastic around each side and tie a knot to secure. Repeat for additional boxes.

SAINT NICHOLAS
Pam Klassen

SUPPLIES: Funky Peach Rain holographic paper, self-adhesive transparency (Grafix); Umber, Strawberry Vivelle paper (Wintech); lossie fibers, pressing sheet (Little Black Dress Designs); batting (Jo-Ann Stores); glitter spray (Krylon); satin tape (Lineco); brads (SnapArts); album (Mrs. Grossman's); buckle (Creative Imaginations); foam adhesive (Therm O Web)

Create your own glitter, fuzzy and glossy paper

Use a variety of products to create a shiny page that exudes holiday cheer and specially created textures. Follow directions below to create glitter background pages, fuzzy paper and glossy fiber paper. Cover the fronts of letter stencils with green glitter paper and back with created papers and holographic paper. Adhere to pages with foam adhesive. Print text on linen tape and adhere above and below stencil letters. Add words printed on transparencies to stencil letters. Mount photo over glossy fibers with brads. Cut and punch belt and back with red paper. Ink buckle to customize color and slide onto belt. Adhere to page with foam adhesive.

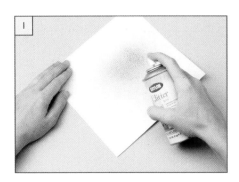

For glitter paper: Following manufacturer's instructions, spray paper with glitter spray. Allow to dry completely.

For fuzzy paper: Cover white paper with double-sided adhesive. Press batting onto adhesive, trimming the top with scissors.

For glossy fiber paper: Lay fibers between nonstick pressing sheets. Use the silk setting on the iron to fuse the fibers.

TIP
Use inks to color batting to match your layout. Allow it to dry completely before adhering to paper.

PRECIOUS BABY BOY

Pam Klassen
Photo: Angela Siemens, Rosenort,
Manitoba, Canada

SUPPLIES: Chestnut Masquerade fuzzy paper, Antelope SuedePaper (Wintech); orange textured paper (Be Unique); Japanese Washi script paper (PaperGami); jaal/apple green glitter paper (Ex-Imp Global); button, buckle (Junkitz); rhinestone hearts (JewelCraft); ribbon, brads (Artchix Studio, ScrapArts); letter stickers (Creative Imaginations, SEI); stamps (Stampendous!); stamping ink (AMACO); staples (Making Memories); embroidery floss (Janlynn); adhesive dots (Therm O Web)

Combine papers

The teddy bear in the photograph served as obvious inspiration for this irresistibly touchable page addition. Adhere paper pieces to a textured orange background. Use a pattern to cut bear pieces from fuzzy and suede papers. Hand-stitch nose and mouth with embroidery floss. Machine-stitch the head to the body and sew all pieces to the page. Slit paper behind bear's tummy and stuff with batting. Sew heart on bear and back the page with stiff paper. Stamp title and add sticker letters and hearts to paper strips and staple to page. Add buckle to ribbon and adhere across page. Adhere photo with foam squares.

TIP
When cutting fuzzy paper, make sure all pieces are cut with the fuzz (nap) going in the same direction.

leather

PAPERS

SUEDE
EMBOSSED LEATHER

Leather may not be the first thing that comes to mind when you think of scrapbooking supplies. Traditionally, leather is associated with couches, jackets and car interiors. But like all things unusual in the scrapbooking world, leather has made its mark. Its texture and appearance give it a rugged, natural look, and its ability to be stitched, stamped and burned make it a perfect addition to the arsenal of any scrapbooking connoisseur.

Leather papers can be found in numerous colors, patterns and textures ranging from suede to embossed finishes. They can be easily cut with almost any tool; however, creating a torn edge is more difficult. Leather papers manufactured for scrapbooking will be of archival quality, but when in doubt, use a de-acidification spray. The unique durability of leather papers makes them great for both hand- and machine-stitching. Be aware that once stitched, the holes made by the needle and thread are permanent. Adding colorants such as paint to suede papers provides added interest and texture in that the color becomes slightly variegated while being absorbed by the paper. Suede papers that are lighter in color can be printed on using a computer. Leather papers are inherently thicker and suede papers are softer with both types requiring a strong double-sided adhesive to be secured to the page.

While the idea of leather on your pages may sound a little abstract, the ideas in this chapter will show you the dramatic results of stitching, stamping and melting techniques with leather papers. With some experimentation, your eyes will be opened to possibilities of leather-adorned scrapbook designs.

3 BOYS & A GIRL

Julia— Runs, jumps, and yells at the boys. At just 5 years old she can develop crocodile tears when the world is coming to an end because she doesn't get what she wants.

Seth— happy go lucky and oblivious to the world around him at 9 years old

Chris— very artistically blessed and extremely quiet at 11 years old

Ashton— musical genius, already composing pieces, and artistic at 14 years old

3 BOYS AND A GIRL

Brandi Ginn

Photos: Kara Elmore Photography, Kaysville, Utah

SUPPLIES: Red Flat leather paper (K & Company); Antelope SuedePaper (Wintech); patterned paper (Chatterbox); embroidery floss (DMC); foam stamps (Li'l Davis Designs, Making Memories); letter stamp (Hero Arts); acrylic paint (Making Memories); SuperTape adhesive (Therm O Web)

Hand-stitch leather papers

The rich feel of suede and the classy look of leather combine for a striking stitched design. Secure suede paper to leather paper with adhesive. Using a sewing ruler, poke holes at equal intervals on both leather and suede papers, then hand-stitch a zigzag pattern using embroidery floss. Cut a strip of patterned paper and place it over the suede. Create the title using foam stamps and black paint. Print journaling strips on suede paper and secure with strong adhesive.

> **TIP**
> The soft texture of suede paper requires a very strong adhesive when attaching photos and layering papers.

A TALL TREAT

Kortney Langley, Reedley, California

SUPPLIES: Tan Two Tone Flat Leather paper (K & Company); Chestnut and Sea Shell Hombre leather papers, Mulberry Bling paper (FiberMark); stamping ink (Delta); hinges, red leather frame, eyelet letter (Making Memories); chipboard letters (Heidi Swapp); fishnet, suede lace (ScrapArts); wooden frame (Li'l Davis Designs); giraffe sticker (Paper Parachute); adhesive (Therm O Web); black leather cord; staples; snap hook

Creative attachments for leather papers

This lofty layout featuring zoo pictures includes a hinge-mounted leather panel, leather strips and a leather-mounted sticker. Mount journaling block to background page and staple leather strips between journaling and photos. Rub torn leather "spots" with ink pad and machine-stitch to cream leather. Mount on red leather and attach to journaling block with hinges to conceal. Accent with inked and leather-woven wooden frame. Add netting to the top of the page by adhering on the back. Cut a leather strip, attach fastener and adhere eyelet letters. Attach chipboard letters to inked leather rectangles and staple to netting. Mount photo on page and add sticker to inked leather paper. Hammer eyelets into red leather frame, fit with cropped photo, tie with black cord and hang on fastener.

ALL GIRL HORSE SHOW
Pam Klassen
Photo: MaryAnn Klassen, Reedley, California

SUPPLIES: Tan Two Tone Embossed leather paper, Red Flat leather paper (K & Company); Antelope SuedePaper, Tan Leathertex paper (Wintech); stamp (River City Rubber Works); stamping ink (AMACO); leather cord, brads, eyelets (ScrapArts); double-sided adhesive (Therm O Web)

Age leather papers

A western theme is artfully created with leather papers aged using a variety of techniques. Rub an ink pad randomly over the textured leather background. Cut a tan leather frame, burn the edges, then stamp. Follow directions on page 43 to heat emboss stamps along the bottom of brown suede paper. Age a red leather strap by ironing the backside until wrinkles appear. Age the tops of brads by holding them in a flame until they darken. Print text on a transparency and attach to the page with leather strips and brads. Tie a leather cord through eyelets to embellish the frame. Print information on transparency, layer over leather and cut into a horse head shape. Print text on vellum and attach to handmade tag with brads.

FAMILY ALBUM
Pam Klassen

SUPPLIES: Passion Red and Copper Canyon Quills embossed papers, Peppery Red Serendipity paper (FiberMark); Dark Brown embossed leather paper (K & Company); album kit (Lineco); eyelets (Boxer Scrapbook Productions); rust finish (Triangle Coatings); leather cord (Darice); screw ring (Jo-Ann Stores); embossing alphabet dies (Making Memories); stamping ink (AMACO); double-sided tape (Therm O Web); tacks

Weave a leather album cover

Here a photo album is given a sophisticated, richly textured look. Follow the manufacturer's instructions for preparing and covering the album. Use a sewing machine to zigzag stitch two textured red leather papers and two copper papers. Adhere the red leather papers using double-sided adhesive with the seam running horizontally across the middle of the album. Cut the copper leather papers into a circular shape. Cut nine 3" horizontal slits on the left side. Weave with three 8" strips of dark brown leather. Cut flowers from leather and use embossing gun to heat the backside of petals until the leather curls. Attach each with eyelets through centers. Punch hole near the end of the copper leather shape and insert screw ring. Adhere copper leather assemblage to album; add dark brown leather rim. Cut letters from dark leather and adhere to cover, nail tacks in first letter for accent. Ink embossing die letters before hammering words onto cover, wiping off excess ink. Insert screw posts through holes and treat metals with antiquing solution according to manufacturer instructions. Wrap leather cord around entire album.

TIP
Some paper-backed leather paper will melt when heated instead of curling. Test with an iron on the backside of paper in small areas for only a short time to determine the reaction of the paper.

BACKWARDS SHOE

Brandi Ginn

Photos: Rachel Scarborough, Thornton, Colorado

SUPPLIES: Textured cardstock (Bazzill); patterned paper (Mustard Moon); foam stamps, letter stamps, metal letters (Making Memories); acrylic paint (Plaid); ticket ephemera (Me & My Big Ideas)

Create your own leather paper

A faux leather background created with wax paper used in combination with patterned papers evokes a rugged, boyish feel on this page. Prepare leather paper according to steps on page 41; stitch along with cardstock to patterned paper. Accent patterned paper with dots of paint and stamp image on cardstock with a foam stamp and paint. Layer photos over papers and stamp title with paint extending one letter onto the photo. Embellish journaling strips with metal eyelets and adhere to the page.

How to create the look of leather paper

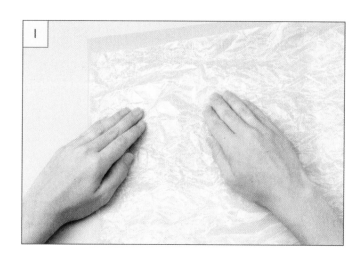

1
Crumple wax paper and smooth flat over top of cardstock.

2
Sandwich wax paper with another sheet of cardstock and iron using medium heat setting.

3
Paint prepared walnut ink over the cardstock surface treated with the wax paper.

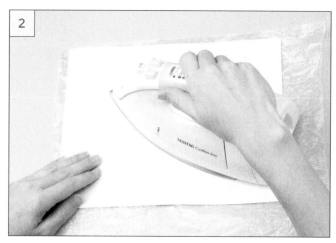

I SPY BAG
Brandi Ginn
Idea inspired by: Marni
Thornton, Mesa, Arizona

SUPPLIES: Dark Brown Flat leather
paper (K & Company); leather flowers,
washer, metal flower, buttons (Making
Memories); I Spy items (Jesse James);
poly pellets (Poly-fil)

Create a leather paper "I Spy" bag

Create an entertaining stitched leather
activity bag kids will love using various
items buried in poly pellets. Cut two pieces
of leather paper into 7 x 7" squares. Cut a
3 x 3" window in the center of one square,
line with clear vinyl and machine stitch into
place. Hand-stitch embellishments around
window. Using a sewing machine, stitch the
two papers together, leaving 2" open. Fill
the bag with 30 items, then half of the bag
with pellets. Stitch the opening shut.

DADDY
Pam Klassen
Photos: Lisa Symank, Reedley, California

SUPPLIES: Double Espresso Cobblestone paper (FiberMark);
contour/coco embroidered paper, adorn gold/red paper,
energy velvet/red paper (Ex-Imp Global); Etal embossed bronze
paper, album (Mrs. Grossman's); Ming Red Empress Moire paper
(Wintech); Cocoa Hemp fabric (Creative Imaginations); red
mulberry, corrugated paper (DMD); transparency (Grafix); letter
sticker (American Crafts); letter stamps (Making Memories); stamping
ink (Clearsnap); eyelet (ScrapArts); adhesive (Therm O Web)

Combine papers

Layer and stitch a variety of papers on leather backgrounds for a highly textured,
masculine spread. On each page, lay first block of paper on background and use
a sewing machine to zigzag stitch around the edge of the shape. Repeat on both
pages with additional paper blocks. Highlight corrugated title and journaling
blocks with red ink. Hand-stitch title block to left page. Add letter sticker and
stamped word. Print journaling on transparency to adhere on right page. Attach
photos to both pages with eyelets and tie with string.

SOUTH AFRICA
Pam Klassen
Photos: Michele Gerbrandt,
Thornton, Colorado

SUPPLIES: Dark Brown and Two Tone Tan Flat leather papers (K & Company); Antelope SuedePaper (Wintech); Chai Latte Cobblestone paper (FiberMark); album (Canson); stamps (Hot Potatoes, Inkadinkado); # stamp, texture stamp (Stampendous!); letter stamps (Hero Arts); style stone (Clearsnap); stamping ink (AMACO, Clearsnap); double-sided adhesive (Therm O Web)

Texturize leather papers

Stamped and embossed leathers create a variety of textures to enhance pictures taken on an African safari. Follow the steps below to ink and heat background pages. Using step three, follow the directions to emboss the stamped image onto suede paper. Use ink to highlight the texture in the pebbled paper. Using a craft knife, cut evenly spaced slits along the edges of the pocket on the left page. Lace with ¼" black leather strip. On the right page, create an opening in the leather paper for the top photo. Back leather flaps with pebbled paper, fold back, lace with leather and adhere to page. Roll the other flap and anchor with lace threaded through to the back of the page. Use double-sided adhesive to adhere to page. For second photo, mount over pebbled paper to create photo mat and add embossed suede paper element.

Mask brown leather paper using torn paper and temporary adhesive. Stamp over page, remove masking and stamp title.

Iron the backside of background page using medium heat setting until bubbles and warps appear.

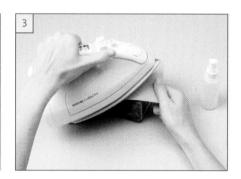

Use a water bottle to moisten the front of the suede paper. Place stamp face-up and cover with the suede paper positioned over the stamp. Iron over the stamp on the backside of the paper using medium heat for approximately four seconds.

TIP
Leather will melt if ironed too long.

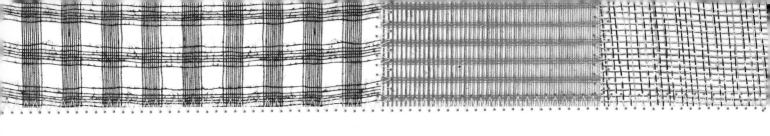

mesh

PAPERS

NETTING
MARUYAMA
LACE

Mesh papers make a dramatic impact on scrapbook pages. Composed of texture, pattern and translucent qualities wrapped into one, these papers have it all. They can be used to soften the appearance of patterned papers or camouflage portions of pictures and titles. When layered over cardstock, the texture and wafflelike appearance of mesh instantly creates a whole new look. The composition of mesh is reflective of nautical and beach themes, but don't let that limit its potential uses. Work with the tactile possibilities of mesh to create distinctive designs with eye-appealing dimension.

Mesh papers come in numerous colors, textures and patterns ranging from delicate fibers to those with a strawlike consistency. Some have been woven with sparkling fibers for additional visual interest. Coarse mesh papers are easily cut with scissors, and straight edges can be accomplished by simply following the weave of the paper. Fine-fibered mesh cuts easily with a paper cutter, but not with a circle cutter. Stamping inks, dye and paint work best for adding color while embossing powders will add both color and texture. Colorants will show up best in contrasting colors and will be more noticeable on a tighter-weave paper. Due to the transparent nature of mesh papers, a spray adhesive will work best. You can also work with circle adhesives and double-sided tape by concealing them under more opaque papers or accents. You will need to use a de-acidification spray on most mesh and straw papers before including them on your pages.

The ideas within this chapter will teach you how to effectively work with mesh papers to transform your designs into visually engaging works of art. You will learn how to create your own mesh paper from fabric and also how to add visual interest with embossing enamel. Experiment with the ideas revealed in this chapter and, most of all, have fun and play!

THE HAPPIEST COLOR
Pam Klassen
Photos: Angela Siemens, Rosenort,
Manitoba, Canada

SUPPLIES: Jasmine Yellow and Surf's Up Blue wicker mesh,
Red River swizzle mesh (Magic Scraps); Real Red Maruyama
mesh (Magenta); chipboard letters (Making Memories); eyelet (ScrapArts); ribbon (Artchix Studio); silk flowers

Encase a photo and flowers in mesh paper

Here multicolored and multiweave mesh papers create textures that work to highlight the theme of the photos. Sandwich blue block element with flowers and bottom photo between heavy and fine mesh papers on right half of page; machine-stitch edges together. Cut out an opening to view portion of photo. Mat focal photo on blue mesh, fold over edge and attach with ribbon through all thicknesses, adding straw embellishments. Sandwich flowers between two mesh pieces and stitch to create tag. Adorn with printed twill tape.

TIP
Without the use of adhesive, mesh will cling together while machine- or hand-stitching because of its texture.

Alexa

Kindergarten

Mrs Nasiatka

You were SO excited to start Kindergarten and I waS So happy for you! You were ready too. The year before you went to preschool and loved it. With your new Strawberry Shortcake backpack and big girl hair do you were ready to go. I think you were a little nervous and it helped that Quin Evans from church waS in your class. Once you got home you were all ready to tell me about your day.

FIRST DAY OF SCHOOL
Brandi Ginn

SUPPLIES: Mimosa Yellow Whimsical Weave mesh (Be Unique); textured cardstock (Bazzill); patterned paper (Chatterbox); chipboard letter, rub-on image, photo corners, acrylic flower (Heidi Swapp); letter stamps (Hero Arts); stamping ink (Tsukineko); brads (Making Memories); black pen (EK Success)

Creative attachments for mesh papers

On this page, mesh elements layered and hand-stitched over portions of the page creatively combine with other eclectic mediums. Adhere white cardstock to a red background. Write title on bottom left corner of white cardstock with a black pen. Layer with mesh paper and hand-stitch into place. Repeat technique in top right corner of page and accent with acrylic flower. Apply rub-on image in top right corner and adhere photos to page. Stamp words on strips of patterned paper and attach with red brads.

TIP

When hand-stitching the sides of the mesh, be sure to work far enough away from the edge so that the mesh won't unravel if you pull too hard on the stitching.

MESH BAGS

Brandi Ginn

SUPPLIES: Starlight Blue Gala Mesh paper (Magic Scraps); Light Basket Yellow mesh (Be Unique); embroidery floss (DMC); charm (Jewelry Shoppe); letter stickers (Deluxe Designs); button (Making Memories); ribbon

Create mesh gift bags

Decorative bags for any occasion can easily be created from mesh paper. Fold various pieces of mesh into thirds, leaving a larger portion to fold over the top. Stitch the sides shut with embroidery floss. For finer weave mesh, stitch sides shut using a zigzag pattern and a sewing machine and cover stitching with rickrack. Embellish the front of bags with charms, tags and ribbon. Fill bags with various items.

SILLY JULIA

Brandi Ginn
Photos: Kara Elmore Photography, Kaysville, Utah

SUPPLIES: Yellow Maruyama mesh paper (Magenta); patterned paper (7 Gypsies); textured cardstocks (Bazzill); photo corners, chipboard letter (Heidi Swapp); acrylic paint, rub-on letters, hinges, tag (Making Memories); SuperTape adhesive (Therm O Web); ribbon (Michaels); staples; chipboard

Fan-fold mesh

This page proves how artsy texture and dimension are achieved when cardstock is combined with mesh paper into fan-style folds. Fan-fold mesh paper and place strips of red cardstock between folds. Staple various ribbons to the strips of cardstock. Machine-stitch zigzag pattern to secure folds onto cardstock. Place strips of patterned paper along the top and bottom of page. Paint strips of chipboard and machine-stitch to the top of the page. Secure photos with a strong adhesive on mesh and cardstock, accenting with photo corners. Decoupage the negative image of a chipboard letter with patterned paper and place red cardstock behind it. Paint the positive letter image, offset on patterned paper and accent with small tag and ribbon.

TIP

Sheets of chipboard can be purchased at an art supply or craft store. When cutting, use a craft knife with a sharp blade and make several passes with the knife until you work your way through. It is possible to machine-stitch the chipboard to your page. It requires a sturdy machine, a steady pace and patience—you might break the thread.

BEACH BABY
Pam Klassen

SUPPLIES: Handmade mesh (gauze); Sky Blue
Maruyama mesh (Magenta); textured cardstock
(Bazzill); mulberry lace border, brads, fishnet
(ScrapArts); stamps, stencil (Creative Imaginations); tags (DMD); stickers (Wordsworth); starfish charms (JewelCraft); acrylic paint (Plaid);
walnut ink (Tsukineko); adhesive (Therm O Web)

Create your own mesh paper

Use a simple process to create mesh paper perfect for achieving the look of a weatherworn beach
page. Follow the instructions on page 49 to create this effect. Cut one end off mesh paper, layer
over the bottom of the page and machine-stitch into pockets along with mesh ribbon. Attach gauze
mesh to the top of the page with brads. Tie netting to gauze mesh. Color tags and stencil letter with
acrylic paint and walnut ink spray. Add photo and journaling to tags and accent with ribbons. Back
stencil with netting and stamp and add small tag. Sew starfish charms on pockets.

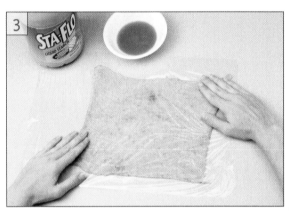

How to create the look of mesh paper

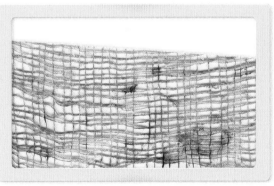

1

Cut a piece of gauze. Place atop plastic wrap and sprinkle spots of ink over the surface.

2

Spray with water and roll to distribute color. Allow to dry completely.

3

Fill small bowl with liquid starch and saturate gauze. Spread flat on protected surface and allow to dry completely. Iron flat if necessary.

jacquelyn

The girls spent the fourth of July at Pismo Beach. They met some other little girls and became fast friends. Finding horseshoe crabs in the sand was a real treasure. 2004

MY STUFF

Kortney Langley,
Reedley, California

SUPPLIES: Natural/Silver Whimsical Weave mesh (Be Unique); Dark Blue Nest Maruyama mesh (Magenta); red mesh (Magic Mesh); acrylic tags, letters (Heidi Grace Designs); metal letters (Making Memories); flower brads (Karen Foster Design); wire (Artistic Wire); brads, rectangle clips (ScrapArts); adhesive (Therm O Web); flower; ribbon; cardstock

Fill a frame with mesh

Here framed mesh paper makes for a clever personalized earring and pin holder. Layer blue cardstock with two layers of metal mesh. For photo strip element, layer red ribbon over strip of blue cardstock. Adhere photos framed with slide mounts on top and cover with self-adhesive mesh. Cut holes for photo openings. Attach brads and flower brads. Hang labeled acrylic tags with wire from rectangle clips. Attach photo element to mesh background. Staple to backside of frame to secure. Attach flower accent with flower brad and adorn with dangling metal letters suspended with wire. Apply self-adhesive letters to complete the title. Add earrings and pins.

INNOCENCE

Brandi Ginn
Photo: Kara
Elmore Photography,
Kaysville, Utah

SUPPLIES: Pumpkin Nest Maruyama mesh paper (Magenta); R.O.C. Taiwan lace paper (Graphic Products Corp.); adorn gold/red studded paper (Ex-Imp Global); Japanese Washi paper (PaperGami); Tapioca Cobblestone paper, Sidesaddle Hombre leather paper (FiberMark); Sand SuedePaper (Wintech); textured cardstock (Bazzill); stamp (Hero Arts); photo corner (Heidi Swapp); pin (Jewelry Shoppe); diamond glaze (JudiKins); spray adhesive (Krylon); Zots adhesive (Therm O Web); ribbon

Combine papers

Repeated circles artfully frame the subject and echo the natural stone shapes found in the photo. Cut circles in mesh, Japanese, studded and cobblestone paper; set aside. Cut circles from red and yellow cardstocks. Stamp circle images onto yellow cardstock with watermark ink. Adhere lace paper to red cardstock with spray adhesive. Arrange all circles on leather paper. Mat photo on leather and suede papers. Accent photo mat with an embellished safety pin and photo corner. Print letters in reverse on various papers using different sized fonts. Apply dimensional adhesive to letters made from Japanese papers and allow to dry. Assemble letters down right side of the page.

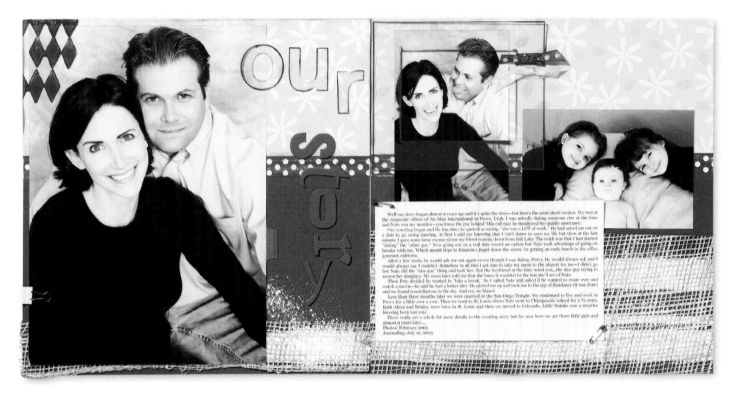

OUR STORY

Brandi Ginn

SUPPLIES: Jasmine Yellow Wicker Mesh paper (Magic Scraps); floral patterned paper (Chatterbox); ledger paper, acrylic paint (Making Memories); clear letters, chipboard letters, foam stamp, patterned tape, clear frame (Heidi Swapp); embossing powder (Ranger); stamping ink (Tsukineko); ribbon (May Arts); SuperTape adhesive (Therm O Web)

Emboss mesh

On this page, various widths of adhesive tape and splashes of embossing powder add even more texture to mesh paper. Place patterned paper at the top of cardstock and ink the edges with chalk ink. Cover seam with patterned tape distressed with sandpaper. Create the mesh texture (see steps below) and adhere photos. Paint the edges of clear accents with brown paint. Embellish frame accent with ribbon and layer over one photo. Paint chipboard letters and place vertically on the page to complete title. Print journaling on patterned paper and adhere with safety pins.

Place a 1" strip of SuperTape adhesive on brown cardstock.

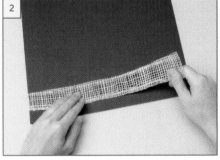

Firmly press mesh paper into adhesive.

Sprinkle with white embossing powder and shake off excess. Melt with a heat gun, starting from the bottom of the paper first. As it begins to melt, apply heat from the top while moving the heat gun in a circular motion.

TIP
Use a cotton swab to paint the edges of clear embellishments to get into all the corners.

metallic

PAPERS

METAL MESH
METAL SHEETS
STUDDED
APPLIQUÉD

Industrial, sleek, graphic and bold—the eye-catching, lustrous finish of metallic papers works well with both feminine and masculine page designs. They can be used to enhance formal themes or may be combined with rugged textures to create a more casual feel. Using these papers to create accents and titles when combined with cardstock or other grounding papers can make a dramatic statement without overwhelming photos. Even incorporating metallic strips or photo corners using a less-is-more approach can yield striking results.

Metallic papers can be found in a wide variety of colors, styles, patterns and textures. Some have a slick, glossy, mirrorlike surface while others look like strands of metal woven together to create a textured surface. Both faux metal papers and sheets of metal can contribute unique characteristics to your scrapbook design. Striking colors such as teal, blue and purple have been added to the more standard metallic color palette of silver, copper and gold to provide a wide range of choices to work with when creating. Most sheets can easily be cut along any straight edge and strong double-sided tape should be used to adhere them to your page. While metal sheets are considered archival, their sharp edges can scratch surrounding elements, so use with caution. Journaling can be applied with a pen intended for use on slick surfaces while computer printing works best if first applied to a transparency and then layered over the metal.

The key to success with these papers is experimentation. Start out using small amounts, try combining them with patterned papers or altering their surfaces. Sandpaper, paint and solvent-based inks are all great mediums to use with metallic papers. The ideas in this chapter will teach you how to create your own faux metal, distress, punch and layer metal and emboss and paint metal. In all, the possibilities are virtually endless.

"The Brothers"

OK, so their MY brothers. Adam (below) 23, Cute and available. Smart, funny, talented and resourceful. Well on his way to becoming independently...well lets just say he won't be "borrowing" twenties from Dad any more. Whatever happened to him wanting to be the "cool brother" (and uncle) who gave the cool birthday and Christmas presents?

Jonathan top left: 16 and starting to date—watch out. He's the residential expert on just about everything you can think of.

Parker top right: 15 and oblivious to girls. Tenderhearted, loving, caring and would do anything to help you out. Always asks how my girls are doing whenever I call home.

LOS HERMANOS
Brandi Ginn

SUPPLIES: Etal Spun Platinum Tint Silver paper (Mrs. Grossman's); Silver Diamond Plate Virtual Metal paper (Magic Scraps); self-adhesive transparency (Grafix); Japanese Riviere-Sapphire paper (Graphic Products Corp.); Ink Drop Hombre paper (FiberMark); letters (Deluxe Designs); epoxy letters (Li'l Davis Designs); Zots adhesive (Therm O Web)

Create an oversized letter with metal paper

Create a masculine design with metallic papers, strong lines and bold letters. Cut strips of metal paper and attach along the top of the page with eyelets. Place photos on page and layer with a frame cut from black paper. Embellish the frame with a letter cut from metal paper and various epoxy letters. Use plastic letters to create the remainder of the title. Print journaling on a self-adhesive transparency and place on metallic paper.

TIP
Print the reverse image of the oversized letter on the back of metal paper and cut out with a craft knife.

Charlotte and I went to NYC — stayed in Times Square. Fell in love with the Met — SoHo — the entire burrough of Manhattan!

New York City

NYC

Famous Restaurants

Broadway Musicals

City Sights

NYC

Pam Klassen

Photos: Susan McFall, Reedley, California

SUPPLIES: Natural/Silver Whimsical Weave mesh paper (Be Unique); Small Whirl-Gold on Royal Blue paper (Graphic Products Corp.); onyx paper (Paper Co.); Silver Diamond Plate Virtual Metal paper (Magic Scraps); Cerulean Blue, Light ArtEmboss metal sheet, embossed metal accents (AMACO); frame sealing tape (Lineco); stencil letters (Ma Vinci's Reliquary); staples, screw eyelets (Making Memories); frame (K & Company); oversized paper clip (Quick Quotes); foam adhesive (Therm O Web)

Creative attachments for metallic papers

Here several shiny metal papers are cleverly kept grounded on a page commemorating a glitzy New York City trip. Attach metal mesh to studded background. Use eyelet screws to attach a metallic strip to the center of background paper. Attach top right photo with self-adhesive embossed metal tape. Add right-side photo and accent with self-adhesive embossed metal frame. Print journaling elements on transparency; cut and apply to strips of silver frame tape. Staple all to page. Cut stencil letters out of metallic circle. Crumple thin blue sheet metal and use a rolling pin to flatten. Mount behind stencil letter openings with eyelet screw and staples. Attach photo to circle with oversized paper clip. Mount circle assemblage to page with foam adhesive. Crimp metal to use as a journaling block. Layer with two strips of frame tape and journaling written on a cut transparency.

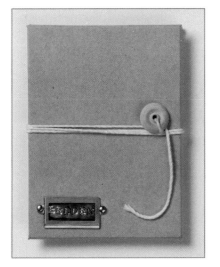

BELDEN

Pam Klassen

Photos: Lori Pope, Reedley, California

SUPPLIES: Copper Medium and Brass Light ArtEmboss metal sheets, Copper Wire Mesh, wire, metal ink, metallic paint (AMACO); adhesive-backed transparencies (Grafix); album (K & Company); stamps (Stampendous!); die-cut numbers (Making Memories); brads (Artchix Studio); heart charm (ScrapArts); white stamping ink (Tsukineko); buckle (Junkitz); double-sided adhesive (Therm O Web); ribbon

Age and distress metal

The contents of this accordion album demonstrate how painting and sanding techniques can give metal an aged look ideal for use with heritage photos. Paint thin metal sheets with gray metallic paint, then ink randomly over the top with white ink. Sand areas of paint down to the metal for a distressed look. Adhere to pages. Mount photos and add wire mesh and metal embellishments, using eyelets and brads. Add ribbon to embellishments. Stamp title on metal and emboss dates using number dies. Print text on transparency, cut and adhere to pages.

FLOWER MAGNETS

Pam Klassen

SUPPLIES: Copper Medium, Brass Light, and Pewter Medium ArtEmboss metal sheets, Copper and Brass Wire Mesh (AMACO); spiral (Michaels); eyelet (Creative Imaginations); floral charm (Artchix Studio); nailhead, gems (JewelCraft); bead cap (Paper Parachute); brad (ScrapArts); gems (Mrs. Grossman's); glue (Beacon Adhesives); double-sided adhesive (Therm O Web)

Punch and layer metals

Use punches to create metal flowers perfect for dressing up ordinary magnets. Punch metal and mesh flower shapes. Use double-sided adhesive to join layers. For select flowers, cut the backs off brads and attach to centers. For others, punch a hole in centers for the eyelets and glue gems to the centers. Adhere flowers to magnets.

TIP

Double-sided adhesive can be heated to mold to shapes and small beads to create a super bond.

On this page (handwritten): ok so i remember her as "ash bash" my little sister who stole my candy. Now she's all grown up, in college & an aunt to my girls.

January 2005

A

Brandi Ginn

SUPPLIES: Patterned paper (KI Memories); textured cardstock (Bazzill); paper flowers, ribbon (Making Memories); hinges (Foofala); Pearl-Ex pigment powder (Jacquard Products); Gum Arabic (USArtQuest); Zots adhesive (Therm O Web)

Create your own faux metal

On this page, the design found in the patterned paper is echoed with a faux metal technique using paper flowers. Layer light and dark blue textured cardstocks for the background. Create faux metal paper according to the steps on page 57; vertically affix on left side of the page and layer with patterned paper horizontally across the top. Print monogram letter on watercolor paper, cut with a craft knife and repeat steps for a faux metal look; embellish with ribbon. Enhance paper flowers with faux metal technique and attach with copper brads.

TIP
The paper being created must be the size you plan to use on the page. If you cut the paper after the faux metal has been applied, you'll ruin the finish on the paper. Watercolor paper works well because it's a heavy-weight paper that will resist warping. It also has a hint of texture that enhances the technique.

How to create the look of metal

1

Cut watercolor paper to the desired size.

2

Mix Gum Arabic with water (a little goes a long way). The consistency should be slightly thicker than water. Combine with metallic colored pigment powder using a 4:1 ratio. Four parts pigment, one part Gum Arabic solution. You may have to work with the solution a little. It should be smooth and easy to apply.

3

Using a sponge brush, paint the paper until it is covered. Once covered, and still wet, dab the brush over the surface for a subtle, unique texture.

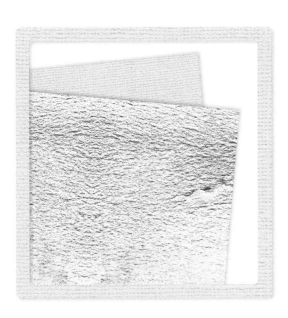

TIP

Cut the metal for the top of the box the width that is needed but keep the length longer. Crimping the metal will cause it to shrink so allowances will need to be made. This metal is very soft, so once crimped it's easy to cut with a craft knife. Tape and sheet adhesives work best with metal.

BLESS YOU

Brandi Ginn

SUPPLIES: Blue mulberry metallic paper (Paper Palette); Aluminum Light ArtEmboss metal sheets (AMACO); patterned paper (7 Gypsies); metal tags, paint (Making Memories); letter stamps (Hero Arts); SuperTape, sheet adhesive (Therm O Web); crimper; brads

Dress up a tissue box

Here an eclectic combination of metallic mediums creates an artistic tissue box. Adhere patterned paper to top half of tissue box with sheet adhesive. Place self-adhesive metallic mulberry paper on the bottom half. Cut strips of metal and run them through a handheld crimper; adhere around the box with tape adhesive. Place crimped metal over the top of the box. From the inside of the box, trace the circle from the top of the box onto the metal; remove the box. With a craft knife cut the circle like a pie with a series of Xs. Adhere the metal to the top of the box and fold pie shapes into the center and secure with tape.

SNAPSHOTS OF ANTARCTICA

Pam Klassen
Photos: Gordon Gerbrandt, Broomfield, Colorado

SUPPLIES: Blue Cordella textured paper (Wintech); leaflet/blue studded paper (Ex-Imp Global); wire mesh, metal, metal ink, metallic finish (AMACO); Blue Mulberry Metallic paper (Paper Palette); Funky Silver Sequins holographic paper, transparency (Grafix); Starlight Blue Gala mesh (Magic Scraps); blue/white mesh (source unknown); Etal Spun Stainless Steel paper (Mrs. Grossman's); Blue Beaded Star Embellished paper (Creative Imaginations); Blue Plaid Maruyama paper (Magenta); Ocean Blue straw paper (Be Unique); slide mounts (Design Originals); stamps (Making Memories, Ma Vinci's Reliquary); metal words (K & Company); brads (ScrapArts); stamping ink (Clearsnap); staples (Making Memories); adhesive (Therm O Web)

Combine papers

A mix of various blue and silver papers and metals helps reflect the theme of the cold arctic climate featured in the photos. Colorize slide mounts with metallic finish and rub. Attach papers behind slide openings and staple slides together. Crop and adhere photos to transparency background. Add slide mount assemblage to page. Stamp title on metal and attach to page with eyelets. Rub ink into embossed letters on metallic words. Allow to dry, then rub off excess paint. Affix self-adhesive words to page.

MABRY MILL

Pam Klassen

Photos: Karen Gerbrandt,
Broomfield, Colorado

SUPPLIES: Spun Copper and Spun Bronze Etal, Verdigris Tint Silver Etal papers (Mrs. Grossman's); Copper Medium ArtEmboss metal, coper metal mesh, wire mesh (AMACO); Mulberry Metal (Paper Palette); letter stencil (Crafters Workshop); brads (Artchix Studio); glue (Beacon Adhesives); adhesive (Therm O Web); leather alphabet dies

Emboss and paint metal

In this spread, embossed, painted and ink-treated metal leaves re-create the beautiful colors of fall. Cut contrasting strip of metallic paper for border for each page. Cut leaves from copper metal and follow steps below to emboss and create negative images. Create metal mesh leaves using directions below. Gently bend and curl mesh leaves to create dimension; attach to page with brads. Sew torn metallic papers to page and attach photos with adhesive dots. Punch title from textured metal with leather alphabet dies. Follow instructions to create photo corners; attach to photo. Print journaling on a transparency and adhere to page. Use letter template and pen to add date to page.

1

For metal leaves: Draw small leaves on metal. Cut out and follow step 3 to emboss veins. Mark leaf placement on spun metal border and cut out pieces. Cut metal leaves in half. Glue to page.

2

For inked metal mesh leaves: Use clip art as pattern to cut large leaves from metal mesh. Rub ink across surface to apply random color. Spray painted portions of leaves with transparent color.

3

For embossed metal mesh leaves: Place leaves on craft foam and use embossing stylus to draw vein lines.

4

For photo corners: Punch small square in metal. Position larger square punch over small square and re-punch to create a frame. Glue square of wire mesh to the back of frame. Cut in half diagonally to create photo corners.

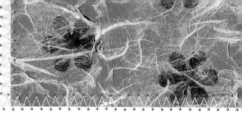

natural

PAPERS

HANDMADE
MULBERRY

You won't be able to keep your hands off natural papers for their ultra-rich texture and dimension. With every fold and tear, you'll add instant beauty and the feel of nature to your scrapbook pages. Handmade papers can have a nubby texture and can be embedded with real flowers and leaves perfect for numerous themes. Take care when working with natural papers, as they are generally lightweight and can fold, wrinkle and tear easily.

Mulberry papers have long fibers running in all directions throughout the paper. They come in a large variety of weights and textures. They are easy to cut with scissors or a paper trimmer but pose a challenge for tearing. You may wish to try tearing against a ruler, cutting long fibers as needed or drawing a line on the paper with a wet brush to aid with pulling the paper apart. Both techniques can produce beautiful fuzzy edges, a trademark of mulberry papers. Look for natural papers that are acid-free archival quality. You may adhere these papers by machine- or hand-stitching, spray adhesive, double-sided tape or sparsely applied glue. Tape runners and adhesive dots can pull fibers from the papers. Natural papers are very porous and absorb colorants that quickly spread. Experiment to find a desired look for paints and inks. Stamped images work best if heat embossed. Hand and computer journaling may pose a challenge with mulberry because of porous fibers, but both can be applied to natural papers.

Try folding and layering these papers to create inspiring artwork that is truly your own no matter the kind of project.

SWEET SISTER

Pam Klassen
Photos: Ryan Watamura,
Reedley, California

SUPPLIES: Double-sided mulberry (Pulsar Paper); green Jute Stickyback paper (Paper Palette); handmade paper (DecoArt); sticker (Paper Parachute); chipboard letters (Heidi Swapp); black bookbinding tape (Lineco); ribbon (ScrapArts); leaf (Artchix Studio); stamps (Making Memories); opalite stamping ink (Tsukineko); Cridgeware tag (Cridge); metal art (K & Company); adhesive dots (Therm O Web); reed

Tear and layer mulberry paper

The feathered edges of torn mulberry papers create beautiful layers of color to enhance transparent stickers. Tear and layer mulberry paper on a double-sided mulberry background. Place torn mulberry pieces under floral-patterned transparent stickers. Attach photos with black bookbinding tape. Cover chipboard letters with self-adhesive mulberry paper; treat with ink. Hang title block from reed with mulberry tabs. Follow instructions on page 65 to create the handmade paper title element. Attach to journaling block. Cover Cridgeware tag with mulberry and attach metal embellishment.

GOLF
Brandi Ginn
Photos: Kara Elmore Photography, Kaysville, Utah

SUPPLIES: Thai Screenprinted Unryu Climbing Vines Green mulberry (Graphic Products Corp.); Verdigreen Cobblestone paper (FiberMark); Celery Waffle textured cardstock (Creative Imaginations); halo emboss/white paper (Ex-Imp Global); patterned paper (KI Memories); textured cardstock (Bazzill); hinges, paint (Making Memories); foam stamp (Heidi Swapp); letter stamps (Li'l Davis Designs); stamping ink (Tsukineko); adhesive (Therm O Web); brads

Creative attachments for natural papers

An anchoring border featuring various papers, styles of stitching and subtly placed hinge accents prevents the photos from becoming overwhelmed. Cut various strips of paper; ink the edges and layer across the bottom of the page. Attach with various sewing stitches and accent with hinges. Cover seams of paper with a strip of textured green cardstock. Cut patterned mulberry paper and place in top left corner; attach with a row of white brads. Adhere photos. Create stamped images and title with foam stamps and paint.

LOVE AT FIRST SIGHT

Brandi Ginn

Photos: Kara Elmore Photography, Kaysville, Utah

SUPPLIES: Mulberry paper, handmade paper (DMD); Thai Lace Lightweight Spiral paper (Graphic Products Corp.); textured cardstock (Bazzill); patterned paper, rub-on words, acrylic paint (Making Memories); foam stamp, acrylic flowers (Heidi Swapp); gem crystals (Mrs. Grossman's); adhesive (Therm O Web)

Print a photo on handmade paper

The fragile papers used in this design reflect the delicate life of the newborn baby featured. Stitch turquoise paper to striped paper using a sewing machine. Place lace paper on one side and adhere with spray adhesive. Layer with mulberry paper and use a machine with a zigzag stitch to secure into place. Mat photo on cardstock and paint the edges. Print second photo on handmade paper and adhere with circle adhesive. Create the title with rub-on words and stamp a heart shape with a foam stamp and acrylic paint. Accent with acrylic flowers and rhinestones.

G KIDS

Brandi Ginn

SUPPLIES: CD tin (Wal-Mart); cardstock (Bazzill); mulberry paper (DMD); rice paper (Magenta); foam stamp (Heidi Swapp); flower punch (EK Success); stamping ink (Tsukineko); jump rings (Making Memories); letter stickers (Deluxe Designs); photo corners (Canson)

Alter a CD tin

An enhanced tin CD case makes for a great project and conversation piece. Cover CD tin with cardstock and layer with rice paper, ribbon and photo. Cut circles from cardstock and bind with jump rings to create the pages of the book. Ink the edges of the papers with black ink and embellish the pages with mulberry papers, stamped images, punched shapes and photos.

Allison is fortunate to see her Grandma Friesen often, Katie cherishes her time because she lives so far away, but time spent with Grandma's girl's is special to all of them.

together

GRANDMA'S GIRLS

Pam Klassen

Photos: Chelle Sugimoto, Reedley, California

SUPPLIES: Paper Perfect, paint, accents (DecoArt); acrylic letters, squares (Heidi Grace Designs); stickers (Me & My Big Ideas, Mrs. Grossman's, Wordsworth); ribbon (ScrapArts, Michaels); textured cardstock (Bazzill); acrylic word (Li'l Davis Designs); glitter (Stampendous!); adhesive (Therm O Web)

Create your own handmade paper

Here the look of handmade paper is re-created for a quick and easy way to personalize the layout. Follow the instructions on page 65 to create the handmade page with inlaid letters. After removing the letters, back the title feature with mulberry paper. Crop one photo into a circle, mount along with focal photo and adhere each to page. Tie ribbons to page. Create "G" by filling a letter template with Paper Perfect. Punch out once dry, paint black and tie with ribbon. Add letter stickers, journaling and acrylic word. Mount page on cardstock.

How to create the look of handmade paper

1

Place 8½ x 11" paper inside 12 x 12" page protector. Determine placement of acrylic title and squares and affix to the outside of page protector.

2

Mix Paper Perfect with acrylic paints until desired color is achieved. Using a palette knife, spread Paper Perfect thinly over the entire 8½ x 11" page, making sure to cover all areas around and between letters.

3

Place petals and shredded newspaper on top of wet paper and gently pat down. Sprinkle glitter near the top of the page to accent.

4

Once completely dry, peel paper off page protector. Remove letters and squares, loosening areas around letters with a craft knife if needed.

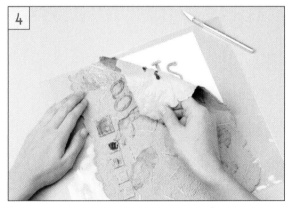

TIP
If the paper warps, mist it lightly with water and weight down until completely dry.

SPIRIT OF LOVE
Pam Klassen

SUPPLIES: Green Japanese Washi papers (PaperGami); energy velvet/black, leaflet gold/black, foil paper/turquoise, sparkle/pista green papers (Ex-Imp Global); CraftGrass Summer Grass paper (Wintech); Tribal Green, Thai Screenprinted Unryu Climbing Vines Green mulberry, Lace-Sky Blue/Green paper (Graphic Products Corp.); Pasture plastic paper (Jennifer Collection); adhesive (Krylon)

Combine papers

Combine natural papers with a mix of prints and textures for a striking handcut collage. Handcut letters from various papers. Print text on papers and cut into shapes. Assemble various shapes of cut papers on background until a pleasing arrangement is achieved. Pick up each piece carefully without disturbing the layout and apply spray adhesive to the back; secure the collage in place. Punch small circles and adhere to layout. Add photo.

MY THOUGHTS AND DREAMS
Pam Klassen

SUPPLIES: Sea Green Stickyback mulberry paper (Paper Palette); Thai Mango-Olive, brown Zambezi tissue paper, Celery Crystallized Mica (Graphic Products Corp.); stickers (American Crafts, Creative Imaginations, Pebbles, Wordworth); key charm (7 Gypsies); lock, feathers (Artchix Studio); brad, string (ScrapArts); spray adhesive (Krylon); double-sided adhesive (Therm O Web)

Tear and layer natural papers

This journal is given a homespun look with the soft torn edges and natural fibers of handmade papers. Remove front cover from spiral-bound journal. Cover with self-adhesive mulberry paper. Tear natural paper and layer over outside edge. Tear handmade tissue paper and adhere to bound side. Cut through all holes using a craft knife. Apply stickers on the cover and wrap with string, adding key. Make small pocket from handmade mica paper. Add stickers and metal lock. Adhere feathers behind pocket and add transparency inside pocket.

BUNNY FRIEND

Brandi Ginn

SUPPLIES: Paper (Rives BFK); Thai Printable Unryu mulberry paper (Graphic Products Corp.); patterned paper (Chatterbox); textured cardstock (Bazzill); photo corner, clear flower, label frame (Heidi Swapp); rub-on letters, ribbon, acrylic paint, stamp, safety pin (Making Memories); iron-on letters (SEI); rhinestone (JewelCraft); stamping ink (Tsukineko); twill tape (Creek Bank Creations); key ring (Jewelry Shoppe); brads (Lasting Impressions); gel medium (Golden); adhesive (Therm O Web)

Peel mulberry paper

In this design, the repetitive use of patterned paper strips carries the eye across each page while the expansion of twill tape unifies the design. Follow the steps below to create peeled mulberry. Ink the edges of cardstock and layer over the peeled mulberry. Randomly place strips of patterned paper on cardstock and layer with photos. Accent with twill tape across the top and bottom of each page, adding a ribbon-adorned key ring to one strip. Create title with iron-on letters, rub-on letters and a painted label frame.

Roughly paint the top of paper; allow to dry. Stamp image with a darker shade of paint and let dry.

Apply a coat of gel medium to painted pattern and quickly cover with mulberry paper; smooth flat with a brayer. There should be enough gel medium on the painted image to soak into the mulberry paper but not too much that the mulberry paper slides around.

Work quickly to gently rub the mulberry paper and peel it away before it dries, paying particular attention to seams and edges of paper.

TIP
This is a great technique for using scraps of mulberry paper. Try combining or layering colors for an entirely new look. If layering colors, allow gel medium to dry in between each color.

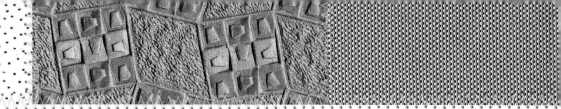

textured

PAPERS

CORRUGATED

EMBOSSED

Wavy, bumpy, nubby and embossed—the numerous surfaces of textured papers simply beg to be touched and admired. Their patterns are striking and subtly add dimension and character to designs without overwhelming the featured photos. The richness of textured papers can take on entirely new looks when enhanced with ink, paint and chalk, rendering the possibilities for their uses virtually endless.

Textured papers come in an array of patterns and colors, each lending a unique element to scrapbook design. Corrugated papers have a rough texture and stiff quality, almost like cardboard. You can alter the appearance of the texture by adding color to the raised or sunken portions of the paper. Cobblestone papers can have a distinctive small pattern that works well in combination with more boldly patterned papers. Embossed papers are typically monochromatic in color and have intricate patterns that can be enhanced by using a contrasting colorant. Each paper, if intended for use in scrapbooks, can safely be used in your projects and will effectively receive colorants without complication. Textured papers, with the exception of corrugated papers, can be cut with any straight-edge cutter in addition to circle and shape cutters. For cutting a circle from corrugated paper, try working from the backside of the paper first to create the initial cut, then finish with scissors. As these papers are lacking in smooth surfaces, only glutinous adhesive, adhesive dots and strong double-sided tape will be successful.

Discover for yourself the vast array of possibilities of working with textured papers. The ideas in this chapter will teach you how to create your own texture using plastic wrap and bubble pack in addition to effective layering and collage techniques.

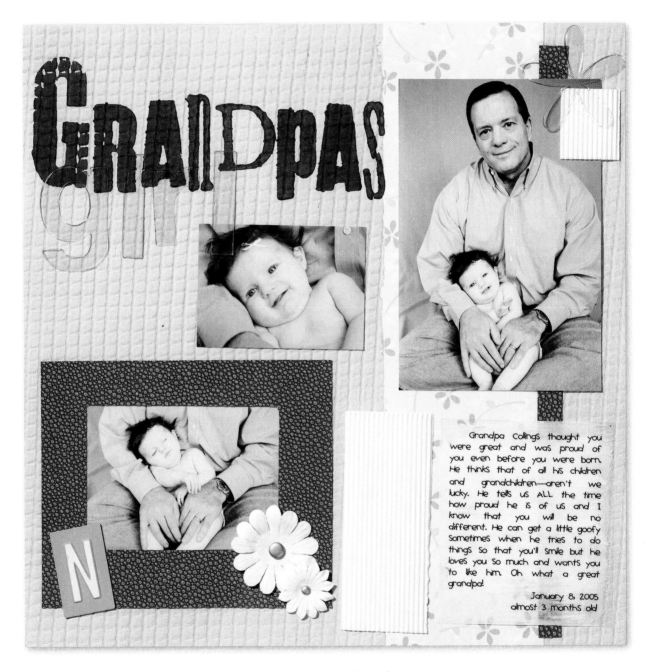

GRANDPA'S GIRL
Brandi Ginn

SUPPLIES: Celery Waffle textured cardstock (Creative Imaginations); Blueberry Fizz Cobblestone paper (FiberMark); corrugated paper (DMD); patterned paper (Chatterbox); foam stamps (Li'l Davis Designs, Making Memories); letter, paper flowers, brad (Making Memories); clear letters, clear flowers (Heidi Swapp); Zots adhesive (Therm O Web)

Layer textures

This design is all about texture. Tear patterned paper along a straight-edge ruler and layer with cobblestone paper; adhere to textured background. Cut a frame from cobblestone paper, place over photo and embellish with paper flowers and plastic letter. Create title with foam letter stamps and acrylic letters. Print journaling on a transparency, paint the back and adhere to the page.

TIP
Draw attention to details in a photo by framing an element of the image. In this case, the endearing size difference between the hands of each photo subject.

Sandcastles and ocean Waves are All Jameson & Tamsen need to get lost in their own little world.

CAYUCOS
Art and Photos: Carrie Taves,
Reedley, California

SUPPLIES: White Straw paper (Be Unique); dusk emboss/apple green, halo emboss/hot purple, halo emboss/apple green papers (Ex-Imp Global); corrugated paper (DMD); self-adhesive transparency (Grafix); stickers, eyelets (Creative Imaginations); metal words (K & Company); pins, clips (Making Memories); glue (Beacon Adhesives); adhesive (Therm O Web); shells; net; mop fibers

Creative attachments for textured papers

On this page, a variety of attachments reflective of a beach theme help pull together assorted textured papers. Layer woven white paper over a green background. Mat photos on textured papers and adhere to page with pins and a clip. Use an ink pad to colorize the tops of the journaling and title blocks. Adhere to page and embellish with pin inserted through textured paper circle. Re-create the look of weathered rope with tied mop fibers accented with clips, seashells, metal words and eyelets. Apply letter stickers for the title and add journaling printed on transparency. Glue net to page.

FLORAL CONE

Pam Klassen

SUPPLIES: White/floralzemboss paper (Ex-Imp Global); Copper Medium metal sheet (AMACO); eyelets (Creative Imaginations); pigment paint-interference green (Golden); ribbon (Artchix Studio, ScrapArts); double-sided adhesive (Therm O Web); decorative scalloped scissors

Highlight textured paper

Use paint and a brayer to highlight embossed areas of textured paper to create the look of a metal wall hanging. Ink paper and allow to dry. Roll paper into a cone and tape the seam from the inside. Cut off bottom and tape bottom closed from the inside. Cut a 1½" strip of paper and trim one side with decorative scissors. Fold strip over top edge of cone and tape to the inside. Cut metal ovals and punch holes in centers. Emboss the tops of eyelets to change color and attach to metal ovals. Thread ribbon through eyelets and tie on each side.

JUST PEACHY

Art and Photos; MaryAnn Klassen, Reedley, California

SUPPLIES: Willow, Cocoa, Wheat, and Celery Waffle textured cardstocks, canvas tag (Creative Imaginations); Kernel Mustard-Embossed Crinkle paper (Mrs. Grossman's); letter stickers (Me & My Big Ideas, Wordsworth); stamping ink (Clearsnap); photo anchors (Junkitz); brads (ScrapArts); clips (Making Memories); square frames (Scrapworks); fiber (Colorbök); adhesive (Therm O Web)

Tear and crumple textured paper

Added texture is instantly achieved through torn and crumpled elements. Crumple yellow papers, flatten and ink edges. Ink the tops and edges of textured photo mats and journaling blocks. Adhere photos to mats and affix to page. Add clips and fibers. Affix stickers and add journaling blocks accented with photo anchors. Frame small photos and text accent and mount all on page. Ink tag, add sticker and hang from fiber.

WHEE
Brandi Ginn
Photos: Rachel Scarborough,
Thornton, Colorado

SUPPLIES: Green, yellow, brown cardstock, chipboard
shapes (Bazzill); patterned paper (7 Gypsies); rub-on
letter (Heidi Swapp); foam letter stamps (Li'l Davis
Designs, Making Memories); letter stamps (Hero Arts);
stamping ink (Ranger); liquid adhesive (USArtQuest);
Zots adhesive (Therm O Web); plastic wrap

Create your own textured paper

On this page, visual interest is created with a paint-treated background and by stair-stepped title elements boasting repeated letter "e's" as if to say "Wheeeee." Follow the instructions on page 73 to create a textured surface on the bottom portion of the page using plastic wrap and bubble packing. Place three photos across the top of the page, accenting with label tape and chipboard pieces. Place ribbon over the bottom edge of photos. Double mat one photo and adhere to the page. Use liquid adhesive to attach cardstock to chipboard shapes and allow to dry. Sand the edges and stamp various letters with ink and paint on blocks. Adhere patterned paper to an album cover and embellish with ribbon and journaling.

How to create the look of texture

1
Mix acrylic paint with gel medium.
(The medium adds dimension to the paint but the technique can still be accomplished without it.)

2
Loosely crumple plastic wrap and blot along the bottom and side of the page. Allow to dry.

3
Brush bubble packing wrap with a lighter shade of paint and blot over texture.

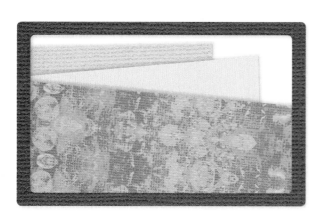

TIP
Try creating texture using all kinds of found objects such as spools of thread, rubber bands, forks, etc.

BUSTED
Brandi Ginn

SUPPLIES: Dusk emboss/apple green paper, floralzemboss/white paper (Ex-Imp Global); transparency (Grafix); textured cardstock, chipboard shapes (Bazzill); acrylic paint, foam stamps (Making Memories); foam stamps (Li'l Davis Designs); letter stickers (Doodlebug Design); chipboard frame (Heidi Swapp); SuperTape, foam adhesive (Therm O Web)

Combine papers

Embossed floral papers echo the look of strawberry stems while rivet paper mirrors the seeds. Cut strips of white embossed paper and rivet paper; layer at the top of the page. Age the edges of a chipboard frame with sandpaper and layer with photos, embossed paper and painted chipboard shapes. Stamp the title on pieces of cardstock and assemble at the top of the page. Print journaling on a transparency, paint the back and adhere to the page.

CONTACTS
Brandi Ginn

SUPPLIES: Floralzemboss/white paper (Ex-Imp Global); patterned paper (Chatterbox); chipboard letters (Heidi Swapp); letter stamps (Hero Arts); acrylic paint, tags (Making Memories); gel medium (Golden); spiral clip (Creative Impressions); Zots adhesive (Therm O Web)

Alter canvas

An address book is dressed up with personal flair thanks to colorful patterned paper and textured paper. Paint canvas boards with purple paint and use gel medium to adhere patterned paper to the front of the canvas. Apply medium over the top of patterned paper and allow to dry. Highlight the design of the embossed paper with chalk. Paint chipboard letters and combine with stamped letters to create the title. Drill holes in the top of the canvas and sandwich paper between canvas boards with binder rings. Clamp miniature bulldog clips embellished with tags to various papers in between each board.

MY BLESSINGS
Pam Klassen
Photos: Kortney Langley, Reedley, California

SUPPLIES: Verdigreen Cobblestone paper (FiberMark); White Waffle textured cardstock (Creative Imaginations); Green Crater textured cardstock (Be Unique); floralzemboss/lime green paper (Ex-Imp Global); Dancing Diamonds/Soft Metallic Green (Graphic Products Corp.); salon — purple/blue, yellow ribbed paper (Mrs. Grossman's); glitter (Provo Craft); Texture Magic dimensional paint (Delta); stamping ink (Clearsnap); acrylic paint (Plaid); pin, flowers (Making Memories); ribbon, brads (ScrapArts); adhesives (Therm O Web)

Enhance textured papers with paint and ink

Brayer and ink the tops of textured papers to create dimension on a fun child-inspired page. Follow step 2 below to partially color white background papers. Cut offset circles in the two underlying papers and a centered circle for the front frame. For the left page, follow instructions in step 1 to color parts of three remaining frames. Ink over brayered area on the top frame. Follow step 3 to create name tags using the same technique for the glitter paper, but substituting glue for the paint. Apply glitter into the groves. Attach flowers with brads. For the title tag, use paint on white paper, using purple ink for "B" and glitter paper. For the right page, follow step 1 to color portions of the middle layers. Spray paint white wash on the top frame before brayering ink in two different colors.

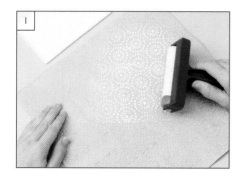

For embossed paper: Apply paint sparingly on a brayer and roll over the top of the embossed pattern.

For textured paper: Lightly rub an ink pad over the top of textured paper to color the embossed areas.

For corrugated paper: Rub dimensional paint over the surface, wiping excess off the top so that paint remains in the groves.

transparent

PAPERS

PLASTIC
VELLUM
TISSUE
TRANSPARENCIES
PLASTIC-FOAM

You need no excuse for adding transparent papers to your scrapbooks. The sheer beauty of vellum comes in a wonderful variety of colors, patterns, embossed and watercolor designs. Semitransparent plastic papers add bold colors and prints while thin and airy tissue papers provide soft, uneven color. Preprinted transparencies can personalize a layout by adding instant words and images.

Transparent papers can create subtle effects when used as overlays to transform prints and solid papers. Make sure transparent papers are cut with a sharp knife or scissors to avoid any nicks or jagged edges. These papers also work well with die-cut shapes. Handle carefully to ensure smudges and creases do not appear on your papers. There are several tearing techniques that produce striking looks—tearing against a ruler or folding to create a straight tear, tearing against the grain of vellum for a rough edge and pulling apart the edges of tissue for a feathered edge. You may need to start a tear in a transparency with scissors. Vellums and transparencies are manufactured to be archivally sound, but check with your store owner on the safety of tissues. When in doubt, use a de-acidification spray. Transparent papers will show most adhesives, so use special tape designed specifically for vellum. Spray adhesives work well, or you can try hiding the adhesive under page elements. Vellum is not porous, so inks and paints will not be absorbed, will take longer to dry and may warp your paper. Use solvent ink or paint to stamp on transparent papers. All of these papers are very easy to stitch, but unforgiving if you make a mistake. Dry embossing on vellum can produce a beautiful opaque design, but this technique will not work on tissue. Folding or pleating transparent paper can produce a beautiful subtle effect, but use a bone folder to crease each fold for a crisp line. Both vellum and transparencies work well when printed from the computer, but be sure to allow adequate drying time before placing them on your page.

With the ideas in this chapter, learn how to effectively use transparent papers by sewing pockets, stamping a card, painting and layering.

WEDDING DREAMS

Pam Klassen

Photos: Angela Siemens,
Rosenort, Manitoba, Canada

SUPPLIES: Watercolor vellum-purple, green (Autumn Leaves); Thai Lace-Lightweight Spiral, Sky Blue/Purple, and Light Purple/Pink papers (Graphic Products Corp.); transparency (Creative Imaginations); sticker letters (Colorbök); pearl beads (Halcraft); stamps (Paper Parachute, River City Rubber Works); stamping ink (AMACO); flowers (Prima); glue dots (Therm O Web); spray adhesive (Krylon)

Layer transparent papers

Layering transparent papers creates a soft look for a wedding-themed page. Cut opening in lower bottom of lace background page. Stamp word in upper corner. Tear diagonal strip from background, and back with blue lace paper. Cover the entire page with vellum paper using spray adhesive. Tear a strip of green vellum and attach across center of page. Cut an opening in white lace paper and adhere to the bottom of page over vellum papers. Stamp heart on vellum near the title. Print black-and-white photo on transparency, highlighting a portion of the photo by backing it with white paper, adhere over page with glue dots. Mount photo on pleated vellum mat. Add letter stickers. Encase a love letter in opening by backing with a transparency. Embellish with silk flowers accented with pearl centers.

Mommy calls you Monkey

You never catch or throw a ball accurately

You are independent and don't want any help

You never sit on Shania or ride her like a pony

You love to snuggle and give hugs and kisses

You love to snuggle and give hugs and kisses

You are loud and laugh at yourself

DyLan

PRIDE

PRIDE
Brandi Ginn
Photos: Rachel Scarborough,
Thornton, Colorado

SUPPLIES: Pasture plastic papers (Jennifer Collection); printed transparency (Creative Imaginations); textured cardstock (Bazzill); rub-on letters (Heidi Swapp); photo turns, square eyelets (Making Memories); brads (Lasting Impressions); adhesive (Therm O Web); ribbon

Creative attachments for transparent papers

Brads, photo turns and stitching keep a printed transparency in place while adding elements of subtle detail. Place printed transparency on purple cardstock and stitch into place with a sewing machine. Layer plastic paper over the transparency and stitch along one side. Attach the other side with photo turns and brads. Frame one photo with purple cardstock and embellish with rub-on letters. Cut monogram letter from cardstock and stitch to page. Accent the letter with ribbon looped through each side; secure with square eyelets. Print journaling on strips of paper and secure with brads.

Paint plastic-foam paper

Plastic-foam paper makes for an artsy accent packed with color and texture. Machine-stitch two patterned papers together for base. Use a tag template and white paper to create the tag top shape and embellish with stamped script. Attach to stitched papers with an eyelet; tie with ribbon. Place a letter template over plastic-foam paper and emboss with a stylus. Use a sponge brush to sweep three colors of paint across the tops of the letters. Accent with label tape and page pebble letters.

ART
Brandi Ginn

SUPPLIES: Puffy paper (Dow Chemical Company); patterned paper, acrylic paint, page pebble (Making Memories); letter stencils (EK Success); stamp (Hero Arts); stamping ink (Tsukineko); ribbon (May Arts); eyelet (Creative Imaginations); tag template (Deluxe Designs); adhesive (Therm O Web)

Sew transparent pockets

Sew transparent papers into pockets to create a soft means of showcasing baby photos. Place photos under vellum and lightly mark placement. Use a pencil and ruler to create a sewing grid for photos and other elements. Lightly tape front of vellum and back of plastic together and sew along grid lines through both thicknesses to create pockets. Pull thread ends to the back and tie. On the back of the page, use a craft knife to open the tops of each pocket. Fill with photos, stickers, text printed on vellum and flowers. Attach gems to the front of page in the flower centers.

IN THE EYES OF A CHILD
Pam Klassen
Photos: Angela Siemens, Rosenort, Manitoba, Canada

SUPPLIES: Pasture plastic paper (Jennifer Collection); vellum-opal raindrops (Paper Company); sticker (Karen Foster Design); gems (Mrs. Grossman's); artist's tape

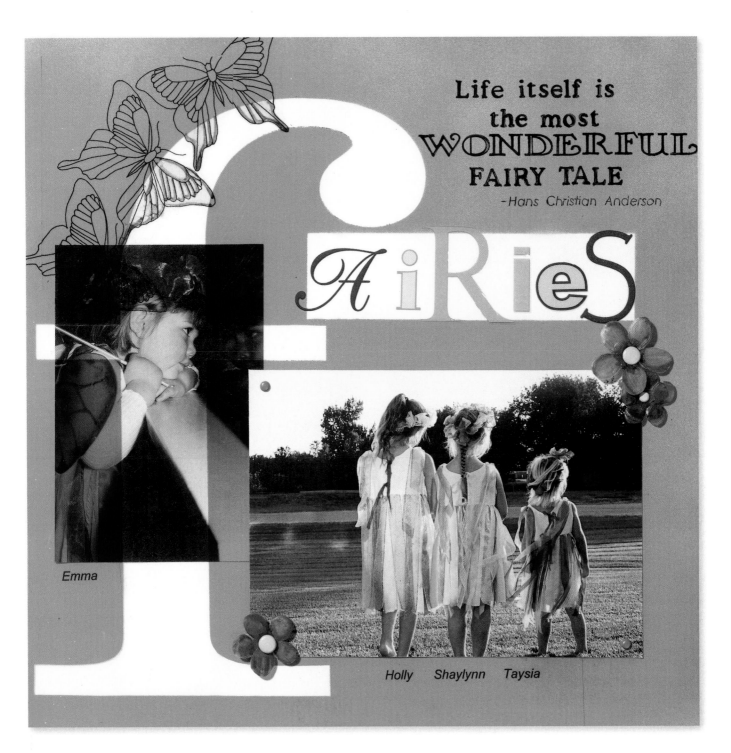

Life itself is the most WONDERFUL FAIRY TALE
-Hans Christian Anderson

FAiRieS

Emma

Holly   Shaylynn   Taysia

FAIRIES

Pam Klassen

Photos: Angela Siemens, Rosenort, Manitoba, Canada

SUPPLIES: Transparency (Grafix); transparent spray, paint, temporary adhesive (Krylon); rub-on letters (Me & My Big Ideas); letter template (Crafter's Workshop); clear sticker (Paper Parachute); pens (American Crafts); Friendly Plastic (AMACO); brads (ScrapArts); adhesive (Therm O Web)

Create your own transparent paper

This whimsical design resulted with the creative use of sheer spray paint and strategic masking. Follow steps 1 and 2 on page 81 to mask and spray the transparency. Add rub-on letters to complete the title. To create the journaling, use a letter template in reverse on the backside of the page and fill in letters with permanent marker. Using pens designed for use on slick surfaces, color in the portion of the butterfly sticker that will be seen through the clear letter. Position and adhere photo and sticker behind letter. Use brads to attach the photo to the front of the page, holding all thicknesses together. Create plastic flowers according to manufacturer instructions and color with slick pens as shown in step 3. Attach flowers to the page with brads through the centers.

TIP
Page protectors will also work in place of a transparency, but are not as rigid and need to lay flat to spray paint.

How to create the look of transparent paper

1
Print large letter on computer and cut out. Use temporary adhesive to adhere letter and journaling block in reverse to the back (rough) side of the transparency. Spray the entire back of the page and allow to dry completely.

2
Peel off and discard letter and journaling block.

3
Follow manufacturer instructions for Friendly Plastic to melt and mold flower petals. Reheat centers and attach petals together. Color with pens.

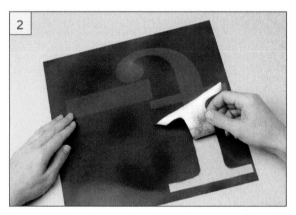

HAWAII
Brandi Ginn
Photos: Staci Langford,
Erie, Colorado

SUPPLIES: Transparency, vellum (Grafix); White Waffle textured cardstock (Creative Imaginations); patterned paper (KI Memories); textured cardstock (Bazzill); acrylic frame (Heidi Swapp); foam stamps, acrylic paint (Making Memories); silk ribbon

Combine papers

For a unique look, the dolphin photo in this layout was printed on a self-adhesive transparency and layered atop textured paper. Stitch patterned paper to cardstock using a sewing machine. Print one photo on a transparency and place on textured paper. Frame photo with painted acrylic frame embellished with ribbon. Stamp title on transparency with acrylic paint. Cut flowers from vellum, layer and machine-stitch to page. Print journaling on a transparency, paint the back and adhere to page.

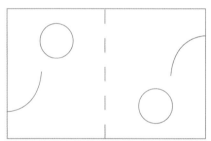

SMILE, IT'S YOUR BIRTHDAY
Pam Klassen

SUPPLIES: Vellum (Grafix); die-cut letters (Ellison); stamps (Inkadinkado, Stampendous!); stamping ink (AMACO); double-sided adhesive (Therm O Web)

Stamp a vellum card

Cut windows in vellum to reveal the stamped theme of a birthday card. Cut out an 8½ x 5¼" card from cardstock. Follow template to cut circles and then fold. On the front and inside of card, adhere die-cut letters, then cover complete card with double-sided adhesive and re-cut holes. Peel off adhesive backing and cover with vellum. Stamp message and smiley face and cut ¼ circles on the front edges for card closure.

A
Brandi Ginn
Photos: Staci Langford, Erie, Colorado

SUPPLIES: Transparency (Grafix); textured cardstock (Bazzill); patterned ribbon (May Arts); photo corners (Canson); file label (Avery); page pebble (Making Memories); SuperTape adhesive (Therm O Web); tissue paper; silk ribbon

Crumple tissue paper

Whimsical texture is instantly added with a tissue paper border. Create crumpled strips of tissue by following steps below; adhere along the top and bottom of the layout. Accent with patterned ribbon and painted polka dots. Print the reverse image of an oversized letter on textured green cardstock and cut with a craft knife. Embellish letter with page pebble, ribbon and clear file label. Frame one photo with silk ribbon and stitch at corners. Frame another photo with a painted and stitched chipboard frame embellished with ribbon.

Place adhesive 1" from the bottom of the page.

Press crumpled tissue paper into exposed adhesive.

Lightly dab the top of the tissue paper with shadow ink.

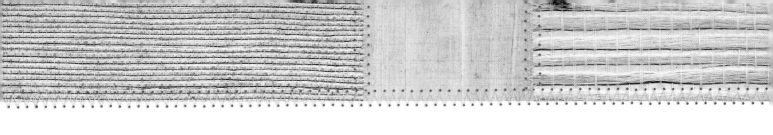

Wood

PAPERS

CORK
BAMBOO

Wood on a scrapbook page? It may sound like a crazy idea, but part of using specialty papers in scrapbook design is about being bold and creative. While lignin is found in wood and is lethal to maintaining the integrity of archival quality, it can be managed. First and foremost, never use pictures that cannot be replaced! You can mat photos on cardstock to serve as a buffer against contact with the wood. Additionally, page protectors will prevent the transfer of harmful agents to photos on the opposite page.

Wood creates a natural, earthy feel to pages and is available in variegated colors and unique patterns. Thin wood and cork papers can easily be torn to create uneven edges that provide additional visual interest in your page. Cork paper is slightly absorbent, so stamped images applied with paint will create unique textures. Both papers work well with straight-edge cutting tools and should be adhered with adhesive dots or double-sided tape. Wood paper can be written on with marker-style pens and cork paper can receive computer journaling depending on the type of printer you have.

Throughout this chapter, we will show you how to work with these unique papers to create original designs for both scrapbooking and paper arts. We've created the look of wood using mediums found at the art store and designs that show unique "peeling paint" characteristics. While wood may not be the first thing you'd include in your scrapbook, give it a try and be inspired by these distinctive and artistic designs.

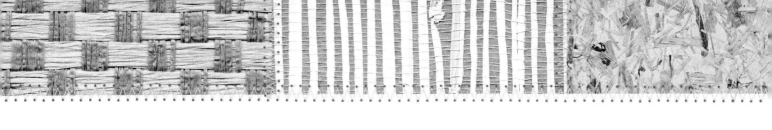

Within the photo layout, handwritten journaling reads:

> You can see this tree from almost anywhere in Erie. It's survived on its own in the middle of the field.

MAJESTIC
Brandi Ginn
Photos: Amy Brasier, Erie, Colorado

SUPPLIES: Egyptian Papyrus-Speckled Medium wood paper (Graphic Products Corp.); cork paper (Magic Scraps); textured cardstock (Bazzill); patterned paper (Mustard Moon); chipboard letter (Heidi Swapp); acrylic paint, foam stamps, photo turns, brads (Making Memories); foam stamps (Li'l Davis Designs); hemp (Crafts Etc.); adhesive (Therm O Web)

Stamp on cork paper

Here the earthy feel of wood paper enhances the overall theme of the page. Adhere patterned paper to cardstock and layer with wood paper. Accent with photo turns. Tear a piece of cork paper and stamp with acrylic paint and foam stamps. Layer a photo over a portion of cork paper. Paint the negative image of a chipboard letter and place over part of photo. Punch holes along the left side of the page and weave a blanket stitch with hemp cord.

TIP
To maintain the integrity and raw feel of wood paper, carefully tear the edges.

ATTACHMENTS
Hinges • Photo turns • Eye screws • Clothespin • Staple • Ribbon

PURE FUN
Pam Klassen

SUPPLIES: Natural Particles paper (Magic Scraps); Egyptian Papyrus wood paper (Graphic Products Corp.); rub-on letters (Me & My Big Ideas); stencil letters, brads (Artchix Studio); clothespin (Michaels); ribbon (ScrapArts); photo anchors (Junkitz); hinges (Making Memories); adhesive (Therm O Web); eye screw

Creative attachments for wood papers

On this page, wood paper-enhanced stencils and photo mats help emphasize the rustic feel of outdoor photos, while a variety of attachments add even more appeal. Cut wood paper to cover stencil letters and ink edges. Back letters with photos. Attach to page with photo anchors and brads. Create matted word accent from cardstock, wood papers and rub-on letters and use small eye screws to dangle from "U." Use brads to attach ribbon to page and anchor photo. Ink edges of wooden photo mat and attach over journaling block with hinges. Use a clothespin to hold nature memorabilia.

To my kids and their cousin Ezra this is PURE FUN! An afternoon at Kings River. Exploring, getting their feet wet and collecting stuff! 2005

LAMPSHADE
Pam Klassen

SUPPLIES: Yellow Straw textured paper (Magic Scraps); Egyptian Papyrus wood paper, skeleton leaves (Graphic Products Corp.); spray adhesive (Krylon); glue (Beacon Adhesives); lamp shade (Hancock Fabrics)

Create a straw-covered lampshade

Here straw paper and skeleton leaves create an earthy and highly unique lampshade. Using a purchased lampshade, draw evenly spaced rectangles around the center of the shade. Cut openings with a sharp craft knife. Mark openings on straw paper and cut out. Stuff lamp shade with newspaper and spray with adhesive. Lay skeleton leaves over openings and wrap papers around shade, adding glue along the seams. Cut strips from papyrus wood and glue to the top and bottom edges of the shade.

TIP
Straw paper is delicate and can fall apart with excessive handling and cutting. Marking cut marks first with a pencil and cutting with scissors helps ensure much of the straw will stay intact.

THE SUMMER WOODLAND FAIRY
Pam Klassen

SUPPLIES: Brown and Green Straw papers, Grass Particles paper (Magic Scraps); Zambezi tissue paper (Graphic Products Corp.); paint (Ranger); ribbon (Artchix Studio); foam adhesive (Therm O Web); spray adhesive (Krylon)

Alternate straw papers

Create an eye-catching background and border by alternating the grain and color of straw paper for a rustic page theme. Cut circles in the border and background and replace them with straw paper circles of a similar color, placing the grain at a different angle against the background. Create a straw paper flower and apply spray adhesive to flower and circles to adhere glitter. Attach flower to the lower circle through center with a ribbon. Punch holes in photo and straw tabs and tie with ribbons. Add journaling on tissue.

MOUNTAIN MAN
Brandi Ginn
Photos: Rachel Scarborough, Thornton, Colorado

SUPPLIES: Textured paper (Rives BFK); textured cardstock (Bazzill); patterned paper (Rusty Pickle); green patterned paper (Mustard Moon); tag (Foofala); chipboard letter, acrylic paint, letter stickers (Making Memories); adhesive (Therm O Web); ribbon

Create your own wooden texture

The tactile barklike texture in this design echoes the textures and patterns found in the scenic mountain photos. Layer patterned papers on textured green cardstock. Follow the steps on page 89 to create bark paper. Place on left side of the page. Place photos throughout the page. Cut a frame from chipboard and create bark texture, then layer frame over one photo. Paint chipboard letter and embellish with letter stickers. Write journaling on a walnut ink tag.

How to create the
look of faux bark

1
Apply textured paste to a sea sponge. Gently blot the paper, creating as many high peaks as possible. (The more paste on the sponge, the more likely you'll get larger peaks.)

2
While the paste is still wet, use a palette knife to gently smooth the highest peaks flat. You can continue to smooth the peaks until the desired effect is achieved, but be sure to use gentle pressure. If more paste is smoothed than desired, simply use the sponge to re-create the peaks. Allow to dry.

3
Using a makeup sponge, apply one color of acrylic paint to the entire textured surface. Mix paint with a second color and go back over the texture. Don't bother using different sponges for each color. You'll want the colors to "bleed" together for a barklike appearance.

PAINTBRUSHES
Brandi Ginn

SUPPLIES: Green Straw textured paper, cork paper (Magic Scraps); letter stamps, rickrack stamp (Hero Arts); stamping ink (Clearsnap); adhesive (Therm O Web); paint can; jute

Cover a can with bamboo paper

A custom-designed paint can serves as an artful and original way to display paintbrushes. Cover the inset portion of a paint can with bamboo paper and adhere with a strong adhesive. Wrap the top and bottom edges of the can with tape adhesive and cover with jute. Tie loose ends of jute together. Stamp cork paper with letter and line stamps; adhere to bamboo.

SUMMER IS MADE 4 POPSICLE SMILES
Pam Klassen
Photos: Lisa Symank, Reedley, California

SUPPLIES: Tan Texture Maruyama paper (Magenta); Japanese Ogura Lace-cardinal paper, Egyptian Dark Papyrus paper, Thai Mango-Olive mulberry paper (Graphic Products Corp.); leaf green vellum (Be Unique); fabric ribbon (MaisyMo Designs); transparencies (Artchix Studio, Creative Imaginations); stickers (Creative Imaginations, Memories Complete); rub-ons (My Minds Eye); tag (Creative Imaginations); brads (ScrapArts); adhesive dots (Therm O Web)

Combine papers

Weave a mix of wood, natural textures and colors to emphasize an outdoor theme. Cut strips from different papers into various widths and weave together, beginning in the center of the page and working outward. Pull strips tightly together as you work. Position photos under transparent areas of weave assemblage and adhere to white background page. Roll the edge of wood photo mat and tie back with fabric; add photo. Apply rub-on letters, rubbing thoroughly to adhere to all textures. To create title, apply various stickers, using brads to accent transparent portions as well as the stamped canvas tag.

SPRINGTIME
Pam Klassen

SUPPLIES: Egyptian Papyrus papers (Graphic Products Corp.); cork paper (Magic Scraps); textured cardstock (Bazzill); letter stickers (Deluxe Designs); tag sticker (Pebbles); tags (Avery, Creative Imaginations); twine (ScrapArts); nailheads (JewelCraft); flowers (Michaels); rubber cement (Elmer's Products); foam, double-sided adhesive (Therm O Web)

Weather wood paper

Paint and peeling techniques were used to create the look of a weathered window to showcase outdoor photos. Follow the steps below to give wood paper a weathered look. Repeat step 1 after step 4. Cut out four rectangles to create windows. Attach nailheads along with a drop of ink at each corner. Adhere pictures to the backs of frames. For background, use cream cardstock and various widths of corkboard. Spray all pieces randomly with walnut inks. Adhere cork to cardstock, leaving small gaps between strips. For title, apply stickers to darker wood and print words on lighter wood paper, attaching names written on colored paper in circle tag. Use foam adhesive to adhere window elements to background. Print text on pink paper and adhere to rectangle tag. Use twine to tie tag to window frame, attaching sticker tag and leaf. Glue flowers to page.

1
Spray wood paper randomly with walnut inks, going over some areas with a brayer to spread ink.

2
Spread random strips of rubber cement down page, following wood grain.

3
While cement is still tacky, paint over entire surface with acrylic paint. Let dry completely.

4
Rub adhesive eraser over painted surface. Paint and rubber cement will lift off to reveal the background wood.

TIP
Repeat all steps over finished surface with a second paint color for additional layers.

Source Guide

The following companies manufacture products featured in this book. Please check your local retailers to find these materials, or go to a company's Web site for the latest product. In addition, we have made every attempt to properly credit the items mentioned in this book. We apologize to any company that we have listed incorrectly, and we would appreciate hearing from you.

7 GYPSIES
(800) 588-6707
www.7gypsies.com

ADVANTUS CORP.
(904) 482-0091
www.advantus.com

AMERICAN ART CLAY CO. (AMACO)
(800) 374-1600
www.amaco.com

AMERICAN CRAFTS
(801) 226-0747
www.americancrafts.com

ANW CRESTWOOD
(973) 406-5000
www.anwcrestwood.com

ARTCHIX STUDIO
(250) 370-9885
www.artchixstudio.com

ARTISTIC WIRE
(630) 530-7567
www.artisticwire.com

AUTUMN LEAVES
(800) 588-6707
www.autumnleaves.com

AVERY DENNISON CORPORATION
(800) GO-AVERY
www.avery.com

BAZZILL BASICS PAPER
(480) 558-8557
www.bazzillbasics.com

BEACON ADHESIVES
(800) 865-7238
www.beaconcreates.com

BE UNIQUE
(909) 927-5357
www.beuniqueinc.com

BIG TIME PRODUCTS, LLC
(888) Buy-undu
www.un-du.com

BLUE MOON BEADS
(800) 377-6715
www.bluemoonbeads.com

BLUMENTHAL LANSING COMPANY
(201) 935-6220
www.buttonsplus.com

BOXER SCRAPBOOK PRODUCTIONS
(503) 625-0455
www.boxerscrapbooks.com

CANSON®, INC.
(800) 628-9283
www.canson-us.com

CHATTERBOX, INC.
(208) 939-9133
www.chatterboxinc.com

CLEARSNAP, INC.
(360) 293-6634
www.clearsnap.com

COLORBÖK™, INC.
(800) 366-4660
www.colorbok.com

CRAFTER'S WORKSHOP, THE
(877) CRAFTER
www.thecraftersworkshop.com

CRAFTS, ETC. LTD.
(800) 888-0321
www.craftsetc.com

CREATIVE IMAGINATIONS
(800) 942-6487
www.cigift.com

CREATIVE IMPRESSIONS RUBBER STAMPS, INC.
(719) 596-4860
www.creativeimpressions.com

CREATIVE MEMORIES®
(800) 468-9335
www.creativememories.com

CREEK BANK CREATIONS, INC.
(217) 427-5980
www.creekbankcreations.com

CRIDGE, INC.
(215) 295-2797
www.cridge.com

CROPPER HOPPER™/
ADVANTUS CORPORATION
(800) 826-8806
www.cropperhopper.com

DARICE, INC.
(800_ 321-1494
www.darice.com

DECOART™ INC.
(800) 367-3047
www.decoart.com

DELTA TECHNICAL COATINGS, INC.
(800) 423-4135
www.deltacrafts.com

DELUXE DESIGNS
(480) 497-9005
www.deluxedesigns.com

DESIGN ORIGINALS
(800) 877-0067
www.d-originals.com

DIGITAL DESIGN ESSENTIALS
www.DigitalDesignEssentials.com

DMC CORP.
(973) 589-0606
www.dmc.com

DMD INDUSTRIES, INC.
(800) 805-9890
www.dmdind.com

DOODLEBUG DESIGN™ INC.
(801) 966-9952
www.doodlebug.ws

DOW CHEMICAL COMPANY, THE
www.styrofoamcrafts.com

DYMO
(800) 426-7827
www.dymo.com

EK SUCCESS™, LTD.
(800) 524-1349
www.eksuccess.com

ELLISON®
(800) 253-2238
www.ellison.com

ELMER'S PRODUCTS, INC.
(614) 225-4000
www.elmers.com

EX-IMP GLOBAL
(248) 347-1821
eximpglobal@yahoo.com

FAIRFIELD PROCESSING CORPORATION
(800) 980-8000
www.poly-fil.com

FIBERMARK
(802) 257-0365
http://scrapbook.fibermark.com

FISKARS® INC.
(800) 950-0203
www.fiskars.com

FOOFALA
(402) 330-3208
www.foofala.com

GLUE DOTS® INTERNATIONAL
(888) 688-7131
www.gluedots.com

GOLDEN ARTIST COLORS, INC.
(800) 959-6543
www.goldenpaints.com

GRAFIX®
(800) 447-2349
www.grafix.com

GRAPHIC PRODUCTS CORPORATION
(800) 323-1658
www.gpcpapers.com

HALCRAFT USA
(212) 376-1580
www.halcraft.com

HANCOCK FABRICS
(877) 322-7427
www.hancockfabrics.com

HEIDI GRACE DESIGNS
(866) 89heidi
www.heidigrace.com

HEIDI SWAPP/ADVANTUS CORPORATION
(904) 482-0092
www.heidiswapp.com

HERO ARTS® RUBBER STAMPS, INC.
(800) 822-4376
www.heroarts.com

HOBBY LOBBY STORES, INC.
www.hobbylobby.com

HOT POTATOES
(615) 296-8002
www.hotpotatoes.com

INKADINKADO® RUBBER STAMPS
(800) 888-4652
www.inkadinkado.com

JANLYNN® CORPORATION OF AMERICA
(800) 445-5565
www.janlynn.com

JAQUARD PRODUCTS/
RUPERT, GIBBON & SPIDER, INC.
(800) 442-0455
www.jacquardproducts.com

JENNIFER COLLECTION, THE
(518) 272-4572
www.paperdiva.net

JESSE JAMES & CO., INC.
(610) 435-0201
www.jessejamesbutton.com

JEWELCRAFT, LLC
(201) 223-0804
www.jewelcraft.biz

JEWELRY SHOPPE, THE- no contact info

JO-ANN STORES
(888) 739-4120
www.joann.com

JUDIKINS
(310) 515-1115
www.judikins.com

JUNKITZ™
(732) 792-1108
www.junkitz.com

K & COMPANY
(888) 244-2083
www.kandcompany.com

KAREN FOSTER DESIGN
(801) 451-9779
www.karenfosterdesign.com

KI MEMORIES
(972) 243-5595
www.kimemories.com

KRYLON®
(216) 566-200
www.krylon.com

LASTING IMPRESSIONS FOR PAPER, INC.
(801) 298-1979
www.lastingimpressions.com

LI'L DAVIS DESIGNS
(949) 838-0344
www.lildavisdesigns.com

LINECO, INC.
(800) 322-7775
www.lineco.com

LITTLE BLACK DRESS DESIGNS
(360) 894-8844
www.littleblackdressdesigns.com

MAGENTA RUBBER STAMPS
(800) 565-5254
www.magentastyle.com

MAGIC MESH
(651) 345-6374
www.magicmesh.com

MAGIC SCRAPS™
(972) 238-1838
www.magicscraps.com

MAISYMO™ DESIGNS
(973) 907-7262
www.maisymo.com

MAKING MEMORIES
(800) 286-5263
www.makingmemories.com

MARK ENTERPRISES- see Stampendous!

MA VINCI'S RELIQUARY
http://crafts.dm.net/mall/reliquary/

MAY ARTS
(800) 442-3950
www.mayarts.com

ME & MY BIG IDEAS®
(949) 883-2065
www.meandmybigideas.com

MEMORIES COMPLETE™, LLC
(866) 966-6365
www.memoriescomplete.com

MICHAELS® ARTS & CRAFTS
(800) 642-4235
www.michaels.com

MRS. GROSSMAN'S PAPER COMPANY
(800) 429-4549
www.mrsgrossmans.com

MUSTARD MOON™
(408) 299-8542
www.mustardmoon.com

MY MIND'S EYE™, INC.
(800) 665-5116
www.frame-ups.com

OFFICE MAX
www.officemax.com

PAPER ADVENTURES®
(800) 525-3196
www.paperadventures.com

PAPER COMPANY™, THE
(800) 426-8989
www.anwcrestwood.com

PAPERGAMI
(800) 569-2280
www.papergami.com

PAPER PALETTE LLC, THE
(801) 849-8338
www.stickybackpaper.com

PAPER PARACHUTE®
(503) 533-4513
www.paperparachute.com

PAPERS BY CATHERINE
(713) 723-3334
www.papersbycatherine.com

PEBBLES INC.
(801) 224-1857
www.pebblesinc.com

PLAID ENTERPRISES, INC.
(800) 842-4197
www.plaidonline.com

POLY-FIL
- see Fairfield Processing Corporation

POTTERY BARN KIDS
(800) 993-4923
www.potterybarnkids.com

PRIMA
(909) 627-5532
www.mulberrypaperflowers.com

PROVO CRAFT®
(888) 577-3545
www.provocraft.com

PULSAR PAPER PRODUCTS
(877) 861-0031
www.pulsarpaper.com

QUICK QUOTES
(360) 520-5611
www.quickquotesinstantjournaling.com

RANGER INDUSTRIES, INC.
(800) 244-2211
www.rangerink.com

RIVER CITY RUBBER WORKS
(877) 735-2276
www.rivercityrubberworks.com

RIVES BFK
www.rivesbfk.com

SCRAPARTS
(503) 631-4893
www.scraparts.com

SCRAPWORKS, LLC
(801) 363-1010
www.scrapworks.com

SEI, INC.
(800) 333-3279
www.shopsei.com

SNAPARTS- no contact info

SPEEDBALL® ART PRODUCTS COMPANY
(800) 898-7224
www.speedballart.com

STAMPENDOUS!®
(800) 869-0474
www.stampendous.com

STAMPIN' UP!®
(800) 782-6787
WWW.STAMPINUP.COM

SULYN INDUSTRIES, INC.
(800) 257-8596
www.sulyn.com

THERM O WEB, INC.
(800) 323-0799
www.thermoweb.com

TRIANGLE COATINGS
(510) 614-3900
www.tricoat.com

TSUKINEKO®, INC.
(800) 769-6633
www.tsukineko.com

UN-DU®- SEE BIG TIME PRODUCTS, LLC

UPTOWN DESIGN COMPANY™, THE
(800) 888-3212
www.uptowndesign.com

USARTQUEST, INC.
(517) 522-6225
www.usartquest.com

WAL-MART STORES, INC.
(800) WALMART
www.walmart.com

WINTECH INTERNATIONAL CORP
(800) 263-6643
www.wintechint.com

WORDSWORTH
(719) 282-3495
www.wordsworthstamps.com

Additional Instructions and Credits

ZIGZAG STITCH DESIGN ELEMENT:
Kit Essentials, Delightful Kit by Gina Cabrera (www.DigitalDesignEssentials.com)

PG. 6
MY FAMILY
Brandi Ginn

The random heights of various tags carries the eye around the design while adding a plethora of colors and textures. Adhere burlap paper to a pebbled background. Use a template to create various tags along two sides, accenting several tags with an assortment of ribbons. Create the title using rub-on letters and foam letter stamps. Use metal stamps to impress the date into copper tag and highlight with rub-n-buff.

SUPPLIES: Double Espresso and Berry Tempting Cobblestone papers, Tourmaline Jewel paper (FiberMark); Egyptian Speckled Medium Papyrus wood paper (Graphic Products Corp.); contour/rose embroidered paper (Ex-Imp Global); Dark Brown Flat leather paper (K & Company); Japanese Washi paper (PaperGami); Hemp- Vanilla Fabric burlap paper (Creative Imaginations); vellum, copper, natural tags, metal stamps (Foofala); tag template (Deluxe Designs); rub-n-buff pigment powder (AMACO); foam letter stamps, rub-ons (Making Memories); shape stamp (Heidi Swapp); ribbon (May Arts); adhesive (Therm O Web)

PG. 6
DADDY'S GIRLS
Pam Klassen

Intricate patterns and serene colors beautifully combine inthis vibrant page. Tear strip from the bottom of the background page. Back opening with torn strips of green and text paper. For border cut four squares of green paper. Cut two circles of pink and green paper and cut into quarters. Layer two quarter circles on top of squares. Add four small squares to corners. Adhere on top of long rectangle. Cut rectangle for journaling block. Ink leaves and apply to page with tape. Cover each side of frame with paper and adhere on the back. Cover corners with black tape. Add sticker to frame and mount picture behind opening.

SUPPLIES: Japanese Washi papers (PaperGami); text paper (source unknown); skeleton leaves (Graphic Products Corp.); black tape (Lineco); double-sided adhesive (Therm O Web)

CONTRIBUTORS

Amy Brasier 85

Amber Denzel 31

Kara Elmore Photography 24, 37, 47, 50, 62, 63

Elizabeth Friesen 22, 26

Gordon Gerbrandt 58

Karen Gerbrandt 59

Michele Gerbrandt 43

MaryAnn Klassen 39, 71

Staci Langford 33, 82, 83

Kortney Langley 23, 38, 50, 75

Susan McFall 54

Lori Pope 55

Rachel Scarborough 40, 72, 78, 88

Angela Siemens 23, 27, 35, 45, 77, 79, 80

Pete Spransy 14, 19

Chelle Sugimoto 64

Lisa Symank 42, 90

Carrie Taves 70

Marni Thornton 42

Ryan Watamura 13, 18, 61

Robert Woods Photography 29

About the Authors

BRANDI GINN

Over the past year Brandi's photography has really evolved. She's made the leap to a digital SLR camera and now works professionally from her home. She's been contracted to do commercial work, and you can even see her sweet girls' faces in photo frames at Pottery Barn Kids stores across the nation.

As if having her third baby one week after *A Passion for Patterned Paper* went to press wasn't enough, Brandi and her family moved to Longmont, Colorado, in the midst of creating this latest installment of the series. As a first-time homeowner, Brandi now has the freedom to extend her painting skills to the walls of her new home and can't wait to work on her girls' rooms. Brandi admits having this much creative energy is exhausting. Sometimes projects get done...and sometimes they don't. And many times the middle of her home looks like a bomb has gone off, and her husband wonders what happened to his wife. But it's all a process and she loves to play. To find out more about Brandi, visit www.brandiginn.typepad.com.

PAM KLASSEN

After many years as a magazine craft editor and author of *Making Gift Scrapbooks in a Snap* and *A Passion for Patterned Paper*, Pam's classic style and creative ideas have been tailored to make the art of scrapbook design come to life. Her enjoyment comes from inspiring others to cultivate their own artistry.

In her busy life working on the family farm and raising two active little girls, Pam knows that there are plenty of moments that don't seem all that beautiful—wiping chicken poop from her daughter's elbow (don't ask), chasing away coyotes in the middle of the night with her husband and canning one more box load of peaches on a 106 degree day—events that certainly did not feel like serene glimpses of life at the time. However, Pam shows us that when those moments are caught in photos, creatively designed and assembled into a personalized scrapbook, the memories they represent become something to be cherished for many years to come.